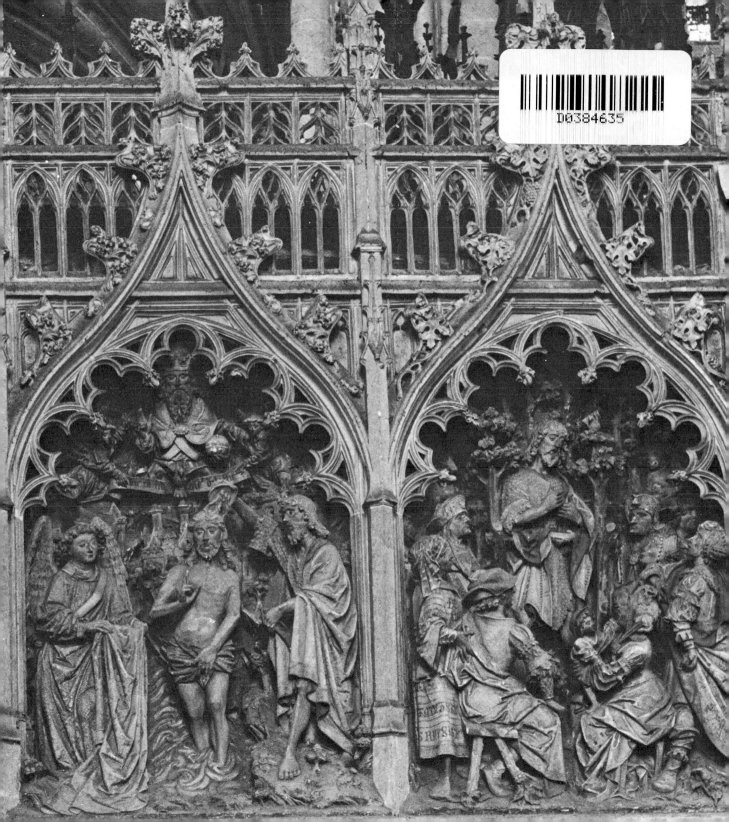

Great Buildings of the World

CATHEDRALS OF EUROPE

by Ann Mitchell

PAUL HAMLYN

Published by The Hamlyn Publishing Group Limited,
Hamlyn House, The Centre, Feltham, Middlesex

Printed in Great Britain by Fletcher & Son Ltd, Norwich
and bound by Richard Clay (The Chaucer Press) Ltd, Bungay, Suffolk

Endpapers: *Part of a late-15th-century screen in Amiens Cathedral depicting episodes from the life of St John the Baptist.*

Frontispiece: *Detail from the painting* The Mass of St Giles (c. *1500) representing the lavishly furnished choir of St Denis.*

Contents

INTRODUCTION

The great cathedrals of the middle ages were created by towns that since the 11th century had been increasing in prosperity, size and independence from feudal authority. As the principal church of such a town and the mother church of a diocese, a cathedral provided protection, guidance and inspiration to all, ecclesiastical and lay, rich and poor, literate and illiterate. It was large enough to accommodate a congregation comprising all the inhabitants of a town. The cathedral of Amiens, for example, with an area of over 84,000 square feet, could house the town's entire population of under 10,000 inhabitants. This sense of community expressed itself in the many facilities offered by a cathedral. Guild business, the conferring of degrees, even buying and selling, all might take place in the nave, the preserve of the lay community. At Chartres labour was hired in the transepts, and the crypt was always open for the shelter of pilgrims and the sick.

And as prosperity and independence increased, so did the size of the cathedrals. At Old Sarum the cathedral completed by St Osmund in 1092 was only 173 feet long; that of Bishop Roger begun in the early 12th century was 316 feet long, while the new cathedral, begun in the meadows of Salisbury in 1220, was 473 feet. In the Ile de France, the vaults in every new cathedral became loftier and loftier, and later, in Germany, the spires became higher and higher. Until town halls began to be built in the 14th century, a cathedral was a city's only visual expression of its civic pride—an expression made all the nobler since it glorified not only man but God. Already in the early 11th century, the monk Raoul Glaber commented on the extent of church building: 'Notwithstanding the greater number [that] were already well established and not in the least in need, nevertheless each Christian people strove against the others to erect nobler ones. It was

The cathedral at Strasbourg rising above the city typifies the many cathedrals created during the middle ages by the same zeal that launched the crusades. They were built by expanding urban communities in which every class played a smaller or larger part.

9

as if the whole earth, having cast off the old by shaking itself, were clothing itself everywhere in the white robe of the Church.' Less than a century and a half later, most of these 'new' buildings were rebuilt. In the area of Paris a new foundation was laid on the average every five years. Jean Gimpel, the author of *The Cathedral Builders*, has described this building fever as the cathedral crusade. It is the cathedrals of this period that are dealt with in this book.

Apart from the quantity of building, the originality of the style evolved is highly impressive. The Romanesque, Carolingian and Early Christian styles that preceded it still depended upon the precepts of classical architecture. Never before had structure been so distilled to its essentials. Walls were almost eliminated, transformed into buttresses, so that the exterior was no longer separated from the interior. Never before had a style attempted to take off from the ground, attaining ever-increasing heights and apparently defying the laws of gravity governing the material of which it was made. No previous architecture had given such an impression of movement, whether in the arcades that travel in an ever-quicker rhythm towards the altar or in the piers that soar more and more effortlessly to the vaults. No style had come so close to the organic processes of nature in its suggestion of growth and in the profusion and casual disposition of its products. These, then, are the aesthetic qualities of the Gothic style.

The technical factors were all inventions of the Romanesque builders. The first of these—the pointed arch—had been used in Burgundy, where it was probably inspired by contact with Arab building encountered during the First Crusade of 1096. Its potential flexibility was not, however, realised until later, in the 12th century. The second feature, the ribbed vault, was most skilfully handled by the Normans, and the first outstanding example is found in the choir aisle of Durham Cathedral begun in 1093. The ribbed vault had two advantages: first, it provided a grid in which to fill the membrane of the vault, which also reinforced the whole; second, by continuing the articulation of arcade and gallery, it was more pleasant aesthetically. The third invention of the Gothic style was the flying buttress, though even this exists in Romanesque buildings in the form of a quadrant arch secreted under the roof of the galleries, as at Caen and Durham. It is the combination of these features, each developed according to the aesthetic aspirations of the age, that constitutes the Gothic style. The evolution was a gradual process lasting some two hundred years from 1050–1250.

Above, a copy of a medieval drawing of the labyrinth at Chartres. Labyrinths were inserted into the nave pavements with a central plaque naming the founder bishop and the master-masons.

Below, a late 12th-century German bronze cover from a censer, one of many examples illustrating the unparalleled influence of architectural forms on the applied arts in the middle ages.

The angle of a pointed arch can be acute or obtuse; it can therefore vary according to the span it covers. This flexibility is particularly useful in a vault, where the diagonal transverse and wall ribs cover different distances, which, if spanned by semicircular arches, produce an uneven crown to the vault. A pointed arch also scores over the semicircular by reducing the outward thrust. The major improvement to the ribbed vault lay in the substitution of the oblong bay for the square bay and the reduction of compartments in each bay from six to four. The introduction of quadripartite vaulting made a neater crown, since the intermediary transverse rib was eliminated; it also removed any need to alternate the design of the piers, thus adding unity and a quicker rhythm to the elevation. Flying buttresses were the last of the three features to develop; often they were added as an afterthought, as at Laon, or replaced by bigger and better examples, as in Notre Dame in Paris. Chartres was the first cathedral where they were an integral part of the design of the structure, but even so they are still in quadrant form and heavy. At Reims Cathedral they are segmental and have assumed the skeletal quality found from then onwards. (Flying buttresses in England, where the Gothic style developed very differently, are rare and never show the same bravura.) Until the erection of Reims in the 1220s no church showed all these three features at once. At Chartres, there are semicircular heads to the windows and semicircular diagonal ribs; Bourges still has sexpartite vaulting, and Laon, Canterbury and Paris, cylindrical piers that are still Romanesque in feeling.

The Gothic style was born in the Royal Domaine, a core of land centring on the Ile de France, which had gradually been acquired by the Capetian kings and where commerce and industry, mostly in wool, had been expanding since the 11th century. But it was not new-found wealth alone that contributed to the rapid development of the new style. This must also be attributed to the learning and logical analysis of the famous schools attached to most of the cathedrals, which drew students from all over Western Europe. An equally important part in the creation of the Gothic style was played by a number of energetic and high-minded bishops, of whom the most remarkable was the Abbot Suger.

Abbot Suger was born in 1082 of a poor family, and at the age of nine was given to the Abbey of St Denis, where he was educated with the king's son. In 1122 he became abbot, but it was not until 1137 that he was at last able to put into effect his long-cherished dream of rebuilding the royal abbey. The account that he wrote of this opera-

The fantasy town running along the canopy of these capitals from the Portail Royal at Chartres (c. 1150) again reflects the preoccupation with building in this period of rapid urban expansion.

Above, four tiles from the chapter house pavement of Westminster Abbey, which repeat the design of the new rose window of the transepts.

tion and the consecration that followed show his energy, attention to detail, and a naïve ingenuity. He relates, for example, how 'Kings, Princes and outstanding men . . . took the rings off the fingers of their hands and ordered out of love for the Holy Martyrs that the gold, stones and precious pearls . . . be put into the panels [for the Golden Altar].' 'The Holy Martyrs' were St Denis and his two legendary companions, whose ashes were the abbey's most precious possession. Suger planned to translate these from the old Carolingian crypt into the new spacious choir, the first monument to be built in the Gothic style.

Above left, a cross-section illustrating the part played by ribbed vaulting and buttresses in the structure of a Gothic cathedral.

Suger, curiously, spoke little about the architecture of his abbey except to say that the new building was on a larger scale to accommodate the vast crowds on feast days. He also proudly drew attention to the 'circular string of chapels by virtue of which the whole church would shine with the wonderful and uninterrupted light from the stained glass windows'. But not once did he refer to what to us is a brand-new style. Nor did he mention the name of the master-mason. He wrote, however, about the symbolic significance of the architecture. The 12 piers of the choir signified the 12 apostles, and the 12 columns of the ambulatory the 12 minor prophets.

Since St Augustine, the Church had been conceived as the City of God described in the Apocalypse: 'And I John saw the Holy City, the new Jerusalem coming down from God out of Heaven adorned as a bride for her husband.' This image, which is enshrined

A perspective drawing of a quadripartite ribbed vault. (A sexpartite vault can be seen on page 126.)

13

Left, the ambulatory of St Denis (1140–4), the first monument of the Gothic style. Built to display the saint's relics to the greatest advantage, its light and energetic style uses pointed arches, ribbed vaults and buttressing—the three technical factors of the style.

Opposite, the Abbaye aux Hommes (c. 1066–1100) at Caen in Normandy, which anticipates the Gothic style both in its two-tower façade (completed in the · 13th century) and in the lucidity of its internal structure.

in the liturgy for the consecration of a church, was elaborated with ingenious and often esoteric detail by the writers of the middle ages. The most common view, however, centred on Christ as the keystone of the vaults, whose supporting piers symbolised the prophets and apostles, as in Suger's interpretation. The portals, resplendent with painted and gilded statues, represented the Gates of Paradise.

Similarly the windows, in the words of Honorius of Autun, brought clarity and were the 'teachers'. For the majority who could not read, they were a constant reminder of the Incarnation and Passion of Christ and of the life of Mary, which was highly embroidered with picturesque details from the apocryphal gospels. The lives of the saints were also recounted in strings of valiant and incredible episodes taken from *The Golden Legend*, a medieval manual of ecclesiastical lore. The actual teaching of Christ was confined to the few parables of Dives and Lazarus, the Good Samaritan and the Prodigal Son, to which a whole window was devoted. Another subject was the New Alliance—a series of esoteric analogies between the Old and New Testaments. For the learned the light introduced by the windows was an attribute of God that possessed an exceptional quality; it was distinguishable from other elements in that it could penetrate glass without in any way breaking it. Finally, it is worth pointing out that stained glass was the principal medium chosen by the Church for transmitting its teaching, whereas in the Romanesque period it had been fresco and in the Early Christian and Byzantine periods mosaic, both media where light has not the same importance.

It is in the sculpture of the Gothic cathedrals that there appears the first signs of a break from symbolism. Here is a new freshness of observation as passionate and tender as the curiosity of childhood. The Corinthian-based foliage of Romanesque capitals has been replaced by the natural vegetation of fieldrow, cultivated plot and woodland. Here is an enthusiasm and thirst to record every aspect of life both earthly and spiritual that is encyclopedic in scope. During this period, the theologian Vincent of Beauvais compiled a series of volumes entitled the *Speculum Majus*, each of which reflected aspects of the mind of God. It was the French art historian Emile Mâle who saw the sculpture of the great cathedrals of the Ile de France as similar mirrors of God. The climax of this sculpture was the Last Judgement, itself another great assessment. This momentous scene occupied not only the central portal but the jambs, voussoirs and tympanum, and was interpreted with the majesty and compassion of the account given by St Matthew. When we compare such

a Judgement—for example, that at Notre Dame in Paris (*c.* 1215–20) —and a Romanesque example of a century earlier at Autun, which represents the account found in the Apocalypse, we see that the difference in mood is matched by a difference in artistic expression. The earlier scene is stylised and distorted, and spreads unrestrainedly over the building; the later interpretation is naturalistic, yet has the dignified understatement of early classical art. The disposition of Gothic sculpture too is more controlled, since it is confined to the important units of the building, the load-bearing capitals (in England, the keystones), and finally the façade and portals.

This logical quality is particularly apparent in the cathedrals of the Ile de France whose basis of design shows striking parallels with the forms of the current philosophical system known as Scholasticism. Its major work, the *Summa Theologica* of Thomas Aquinas, is another of the encyclopedic series of this period. Erwin Panofsky in his *Gothic Architecture and Scholasticism* has defined the system's three requirements. First, a presentation of the totality of knowledge (theological, moral, natural and historical). This we have seen in the sculpture of the façades of the cathedrals. Secondly, an arrangement of this knowledge according to a uniform system of division and subdivision. This is best illustrated by the uniformity in design of a sector of the apse, the whole apse and the choir. And thirdly, these divisions, though related to the whole, should be quite distinct; for example, the cross-section of a pier should explain the whole structure of the church. From the last quarter of the 13th century to the end of the middle ages, Scholasticism was beginning to be replaced by other systems and no longer had the same influence; nor was its effect felt so strongly outside the Ile de France.

In England, cathedral architecture developed more independently of the Ile de France than in any other country. Its island position, the commercial prosperity of London and the political and economic unity achieved by its Norman and Plantagenet rulers, all contributed to this independence. Within a generation of the Battle of Hastings, the conquerors had started to build a string of monastic foundations throughout the length and breadth of the country; these were staffed by Norman abbots and exceeded both in number and in size the monasteries and cathedrals of Normandy itself. The political and architectural impact of this building programme was enormous; to a
large extent it governed the entire future of English medieval

building. The first characteristic was the emphasis on length, which is also found in post-Norman foundations and later rebuilding and partly accounts for the lack of experiment with more centralised plans. Offsetting this is the central predominating tower, an important feature that continues throughout the middle ages. Arcading, plain or interlaced, is another motif introduced by the Normans.

Although English Gothic never aspired to the lofty heights of the continent, there is an intriguing fondness for the vertical. Lancet windows are narrower in their proportions in England than they are elsewhere; sometimes they assembled to form a design of piquant simplicity, like the 'Five Sisters' of York or the 'Nine Altars' of Durham. Linear effects were also obtained by the alternation of Purbeck and limestone shafting in the Early English style. The linear effects appear again in the multiple orders in an English arch in the lierne vaulting, which anticipated all examples on the continent.

Combined, these two tendencies—the vertical and the horizontal—form a grid that was the basis of Perpendicular architecture and lasted some two hundred years. This was the style used in the conversion of the massive Norman nave of Winchester, where a screenwork of rectilinear forms was superimposed to link the component parts of the elevation. Its most glorious monument, famous for its pendant fan vault (a typical invention of the Perpendicular), was Henry VII's Chapel at Westminster built at the beginning of the 16th century. Perpendicular 'survived' at Oxford during the 17th century, was 'revived' in the 18th, and in the 19th produced another national masterpiece in the Houses of Parliament, built to match its progeni-

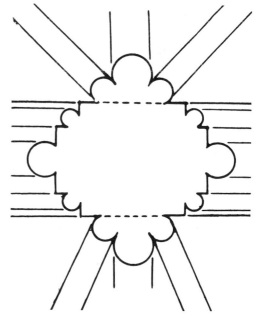

tor over the way. This predilection for the rectilinear is found again in the square terminations of choir and transepts.

In addition to the characteristically English rectilinear forms, a curvilinear tendency was already developing by the 1290s—almost a century earlier than the Flamboyant style in France. The leitmotif of this style was the ogee or S curve found in the flowing design of tracery. In a three-dimensional form, it 'nods' in an arcade of niches around the Lady Chapel of Ely and undulates along the walls of the chapter house at York. In fact, the period from 1250 to 1350 was the most fertile of English medieval architecture—a period during which were created some of the most inventive and inspired designs of anywhere in Europe. To mention a few, there is the Octagon of Ely, the Lady Chapel of Wells and the choir of Bristol.

In Central Europe, the Gothic style emerged more slowly, evolving an independent expression only in the second half of the 13th century. German Gothic had little apparent connection with the earlier Romanesque style (which continued longer in this area than anywhere else in the West) and was largely a direct importation from France. Cologne Cathedral (begun in 1248) is a typical example of an interesting synthesis of styles; its regularity, both admired and criticised, probably results from the German designer's desire to outdo the logicality and consistency of his French High Gothic models. But in the cathedral of Strasbourg the master-mason Erwin invented a new form—openwork—which had only been hinted at in earlier French examples. Here it appears as a free-standing screen of stringing, which rises two feet in front of the façade and covers its entire height and breadth.

Openwork is a characteristic feature of German Gothic spires, of which Freiburg in Breisgau (1275–1340) became a model, followed (among others) by St Stephen's in Vienna (1407–33), Strasbourg and then Ulm (1377–1417), whose spire is at least 529 feet high—the tallest spire in medieval Europe. In time, the effort involved resulted in the practice of building only one giant spire for each church; these, like the imposing belfries of municipal buildings in the Low Countries, were largely an expression of civic pride and rivalry.

Openwork involves a division of space, a basic characteristic of Gothic architecture; this preoccupation with space reaches its climax in the 15th century. For two centuries before, the most common form of church architecture had been the hall church, 18 without transepts and with aisles and naves of equal height. In the

The nave of Winchester Cathedral (c. 1394–1450), one of the most characteristically English interiors. The way in which a network of Perpendicular tracery has been thrown over the earlier massive Norman forms reflects the empirical outlook of medieval England.

Franciscan church at Salzburg (begun in 1408) a polygonal choir, which was deliberately light and airy, was built on to an earlier nave, which was dark and narrow—an instance of the unexpected spatial relationships that are such a notable feature of German Rococo churches. In all the many other magnificent examples, the sense of floating space is intensified by the net or stellar vaults, which spread their ribs as effortlessly as the branches of a tree from the trunk of the piers.

The most striking feature of the cathedrals of Spain is their size; they are vast complexes including cloisters, chapter house and innumerable additions of sacristies and chapels, not to mention subsidiary buildings for the canons. The largest cathedral in the world is that of Seville (founded in 1402). This size and scale reflect the Church's need to reassert itself after the reconquest of Spain from the Moors.

The earliest examples of Gothic architecture appear in the cathedrals of Burgos and Toledo, both begun in the 1220s, succeeded by León in the 1250s, all of which are closely based on French models and probably designed by French master-masons. By the 14th century, a style remarkable for its structural skill was developing in Catalonia, a region rich in civic buildings, of which the masterpiece was the cathedral of Palma. Here slim octagonal piers rise uninterrupted by mouldings or capitals to support a lofty arcade; the same clean line circumscribes the vast untraceried window, which occupies the wall above the chancel arch.

By the 15th century, various national characteristics were beginning to emerge both in Aragon and Castile. Plans show an emphasis on width. When the nave at Gerona was rebuilt in 1417, it was decided to dispense with the aisles, thus creating a vault 73 feet wide and buttresses 20 feet deep. Cathedrals were often double-aisled, and when complemented by side chapels and perhaps lean-to buildings, the plan became square. This feeling for area is intensified by further divisions of wrought-iron screens or *rejas*. The absence of protruding transepts and, at Seville, Salamanca and Palma, of radiating chapels give the ground plan a mosque-like form.

Decoration is either scarce (as in Catalan Gothic) or profuse. The profusion is largely the result of elements assimilated from Muslim architecture, a blending of styles that created some fascinating combinations. The most influential of these schools was the *mudéjar*, the technique practised by craftsmen brought up on Muslim traditions,

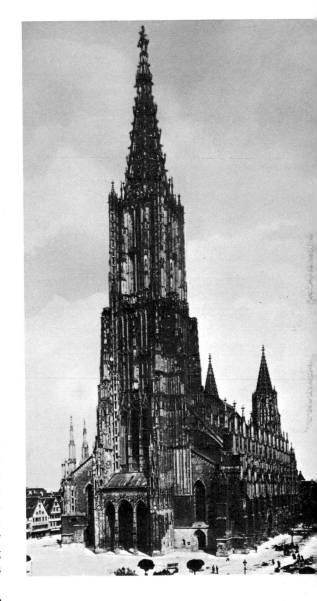

The single openwork steeple of Ulm Minster (1377–1417) typifies the Gothic style in Central Europe. When finished according to the original design in the 1880s, it rose to the unprecedented height of 529 feet.

which they adapted after the reconquest to the Gothic style of the time. Its characteristics were decorative brickwork, patterned stucco designs, coloured tiles and, in particular, elaborate carved wooden ceilings (*artesonado*). Some of the skill and virtuosity of these craftsmen, who concentrated all their art on a world of abstract forms, can be seen in the superb stellar vaults of Burgos Cathedral.

Side by side with this abstract art exists a realism that is peculiar to Spain. Sacred images often include apparently authentic hair and blood; equally typical of this stark approach (which contrasts with the anguished and angular realism of German Gothic) are the early Catalan crucifixes, the still-lifes of Melendez and Cotan and the Dwarfs of Velásquez.

In Italy the Gothic style was little more than a passing fashion. The architecture of Venice, for example, is a charming concoction of Byzantine and Islamic decorative forms to which a Gothic flavour was added. Milan Cathedral (begun in 1387 and not finished until the 19th century) was the creation of successive master-masons, mostly from France and Germany. In Rome no Gothic architecture was produced until the mid-13th century. In Sicily too there were exotic combinations of earlier Norman Saracenic with Aragonese Gothic, which in the 15th century developed into a rich Flamboyant style. Most building took place in Tuscany, and characteristic examples are churches designed for preaching, which are austere in line and material. The cathedrals of Siena and Orvieto sum up the Gothic in Italy, which neither aspires to height nor vertical emphasis nor shows the Northern feeling for rhythm. (The distance between the bays of Florence Cathedral is 63 feet compared to the 24 feet of Amiens. The dimensions of the two are otherwise the same.) Nor does it concern itself with problems of structure (many Italian churches of this period are still unvaulted), relief and the play of light and shade on the mouldings. Instead, the emphasis was on colour, which took the form of mosaic or abstract patterns in marble laid as a facing on the outside walls. (Outside Italy, colour was applied as an afterthought to pick out mouldings and capitals or to draw attention to the sculptural theme of the façade.) Its ephemeral nature is testified by 15th-century Flemish paintings that painstakingly record the architectural detail with none of the colour it may once have had. As for the sculpture of Italian façades, it is applied rather than integrated with the architecture as in the North. All in all, the Gothic style in Italy might be described as an interlude

St George's, Dinkelsbühl (1448–94), exemplifying some of the features of the late German hall church. The net vault and slim concave moulded piers tend to unify the space, in contrast to the piers in front of the windows in the choir, which have a disruptive effect, adding an element of surprise.

between her great classical past and its revival during the Renaissance and later.

So much for national differences. We turn now to features in common, for every cathedral in Europe was inspired by similar motives and built by similar methods. Every class in the community participated. First, building confraternities would be set up by the chapter; members who promised bequests or covenanted annual sums were accorded papal or episcopal indulgences. Masses for the souls of the living and the dead were also said in return for donations. But money also came from the mites given by the little people; Notre Dame in Paris, it was said, was built with widows' sous. The bishop and the canons also taxed themselves, sometimes very severely. Rents too were collected from property owned by the Church.

If the cathedral were lucky enough to own a relic, it was a splendid form of publicity and a never-failing means of unloosing purse-strings. Fragments of relics, such as those owned by Laon, were taken on tour, but more important exhibits would draw pilgrims without being moved. A valuable relic, indeed, not only provided financial security, but also an excuse for added grandeur. Sometimes

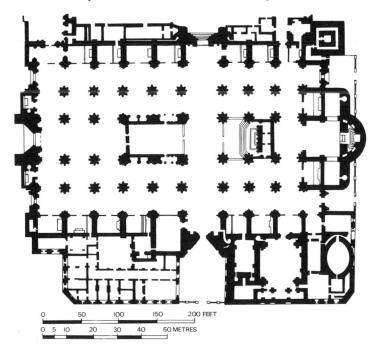

0   50   100   150   200 FEET
0 5 10   20   30   40   50 METRES

This ground plan of Seville Cathedral, with its double aisles, apsidal chapels and sacristies, illustrates the Spanish sense of area as opposed to axis—a feature that was no doubt inherited from mosque architecture.

21

Above, Segovia Cathedral (begun 1522), one of several Spanish cathedrals built in the late middle ages as proud monuments of the recent Reconquest. Note the preference for towers and domes and simple, undecorated cubic forms.

Above left, Siena Cathedral (1245–1380), whose cruciform plan with a dome and a separate campanile (together with the use of brick faced with marble and mosaic) illustrates the superficial appreciation of the Gothic style in Italy. Note especially the lack of cohesion, the emphasis on colour rather than relief and the decorative arrangement of the sculpture.

an entirely new church was erected, as for example the Sainte Chapelle built by St Louis to house the Crown of Thorns.

Labour was often in the form of rent to a religious house or to a big lay landlord, and in England the king could (and often did) press men into service. Labourers might also be serfs who had run away from their lords and could not be claimed by them for a year and a day; or they might be the sons of peasants.

A particularly important skilled craftsman was the master-carpenter, whose responsibilities included not only the roofing, exterior scaffolding and furnishing (scarce until the end of the 14th century), but also the vast bulk of interior scaffolding necessary for centring and supporting the arches of the vaults. He might even be in charge of the whole fabric. So much wood was needed to build vaults from 70 to 150 feet that there was often only enough to build one bay at a time. Construction therefore proceeded slowly. Only when vaults, flyers and pinnacles (essential items of counterthrust) had fully set could the scaffolding be struck.

Glass-painters were another class of craftsmen that played an increasingly important role (and one that presupposed a close association with the mason) in the creation of a medieval cathedral. The small windows of the 12th century are mostly of an azure blue made with cobalt—the colour least resistant to light. During the 13th century, windows increased in size, but the blue (because of the

22

mixing of manganese oxides with the potmetal) changed to a more sombre violet-blue. In the last quarter of the 13th century, the tone became lighter again with the addition of whites. The extra light set off the mouldings, which by this time had developed greater refinement and complexity. By 1300, the introduction of diamond cutting enabled far larger and more graceful forms to be cut; this, together with the invention of silver stain and later abrasion and damascening, converted the early mosaics of jewels into an increasingly pictorial art, though the later less abstract windows obviously failed to integrate so closely with the architecture.

The third important branch of craftsmen were the masons, who on a large job were of two kinds: the stone-setters and the stone-hewers. The setters could not work during the winter months except under cover on such jobs as vaulting. The work of the hewers was more skilled than might be imagined, since they had to be familiar with the various working and setting qualities of stone in a quarry as well as with which was most suitable for vaulting, paving or carving. Carving was done by a freestone-mason on stone that had already been hewn by a rough mason. Lean-to huts or lodges were provided for the masons and glaziers. Originally the lodges had no esoteric significance; masons' guilds developed later (not until 1360 in London), but the profession was one of the most highly regarded in the middle ages.

Head of all the workmen was the master-mason, whose duties included the pricing of materials and organising their transport. It was his job to supervise labour on the site, and to see that there were adequate facilities for holding religious services. He was also responsible for the administrative duties of the clerk of the works, either training a man to work under him or sometimes even handling the finances himself. His principal responsibility, however, was to provide plans and elevations. The ground would be laid out with pegs and string (as it is today) from a working drawing with the aid of a module or standard dimension (medieval drawings had no figured scale), which would vary according to the district or that of the master's origin. Only the ground plan and the elevation seem to have been designed in advance; sections of the minor parts were worked out as the building progressed.

As might be expected, a master-mason needed a considerable knowledge of geometry; as early as 1400 some English masons described their craft 'according to Euclid', whose principles had probably been passed down to them through the translation by

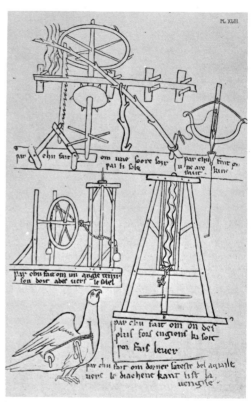

Above, a page from the sketchbook of the mason Villard de Honnecourt (c. 1125–35). It depicts a hydraulic saw; a crossbow fitted with a pinhole sight; the mechanism for a clockwork angel, whose finger follows the sun; a machine for lifting heavy weights; and an eagle that turns to the deacon while the gospel is read.

A detail from a drawing (c. 1437) by Jan Van Eyck, left, of St Barbara seated before her attribute (a tower) illustrates the busy activity of a medieval building site. Note the vast crane wheel seen through the tower windows and, on the right, the mason's lodge.

Adelard of Bath in Toledo in the early 12th century. A century later the Master Mason Villard de Honnecourt wrote in his sketchbook of diagrams, 'toutes ces figures sont tracées de geometrie'.

De Honnecourt's sketchbook was compiled for teaching masons of a building lodge. It is now housed in the Bibliothèque Nationale in Paris, and consists of 33 folio sheets (probably half its original number) with additions and comments by later hands. It covers subjects ranging from mechanics, geometry and practical trigonometry to architectural design; this includes plans, elevations and sections of masonry, as well as designs for ornament, figures and furniture. Sixty-seven different kinds of animals are represented as models for sculptors who wanted to depict the symbols of the evangelists, the signs of the Zodiac, or the attributes of the saints. Mechanical drawings include a perpetual motion machine, one for lifting very heavy weights, an underwater sawing invention, a bishop's handwarmer, a device for making 'the Eagle face the deacon while the gospel is being read' and a clockwork angel, whose finger always remains pointed towards the sun.

If Villard de Honnecourt was typical of the master-masons of the first half of the 13th century, it is clear that the designers of the great cathedrals were far from emerging as a separate profession, though by the 14th and 15th centuries the remuneration of a mastermason has been estimated by John Harvey as at least three or four times that of a fully skilled craftsman. The profession often ran in

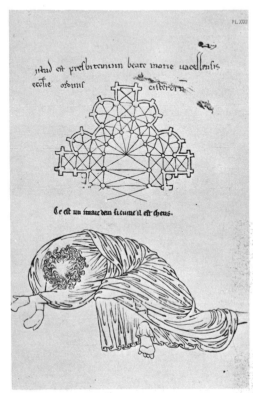

Above, part of another page from Villard's sketchbook showing the east end of the Cistercian church of the Blessed Marie de Vauxcelles. Below it (according to the inscription in Picardy French) is a picture of 'God as he stumbled'.

Left, a detail from a mid-13th-century drawing by the monk Mathew Paris depicting a monarch giving orders to his master-mason—a dignified figure in full-length clothes while the setters and freestone masons are in working dress.

25

families—the Parlers of Prague, the Roritzers of Regensburg, the Keldermans of the Low Countries and the Vertues of London. Masters might be called in for advice; William Hurley of London, for example, was consulted on the Octagon at Ely. Joint consultations sometimes took place, as occurred over the nave of Gerona, where, in 1416, 12 master-masons gathered from various parts of Catalonia. Finally, in Germany there were what can only be called congresses, as when 19 masters and 26 journeymen met in Regensburg in 1459.

Nevertheless, important as the individual designers were, a characteristic unique to medieval cathedrals is their composite nature—the product of many generations. Even the 13th-century cathedrals of the Ile de France, which—most exceptionally—were conceived and completed within a generation, were provided with chapels and furniture by later generations. A Gothic cathedral can never be complete. There is always a statue missing from lack of money or labour, a spire that has crashed and needs to be replaced. Some spires were never built (as at Strasbourg), and at Beauvais even the nave failed to materialise! Nor did later additions imitate what was already there; they were built in the style of their period but in a way that blended with and balanced the existing architecture. Thus even the early 16th-century spire built by Jean Texier at Chartres somehow successfully complements that of the 12th century. The emphasis on symmetry and the precise statement of classical art held no appeal for the essentially empirical approach of the middle ages. From its conception, a Gothic cathedral has a living quality that cannot be formulated by a plan with a figured scale or in a blueprint that decides in advance every section and moulding from the floor to the gutters of the eaves. This organic quality is highlighted by the ceaseless labour of maintenance and preservation. No style is less suited to withstand the elements.

As in the Expressionist movement in art, the final word can rarely be said, and it is perhaps no coincidence that Expressionism should have been contemporary with the publication in 1912 of *Form in Gothic* by the German writer Worringer, who analyses the emotional and psychological motives behind the Gothic style. The striving for the transcendental in Gothic architecture of which Worringer speaks is simply illustrated by considering the physical relation of medieval man to his buildings. In classical times the columns affirmed the nobility of man, but in the Gothic age it was man that was expected to reach towards the ever loftier piers of his buildings.

Rouen Cathedral painted by Monet between 1892–5 expresses the living quality of medieval architecture. The layers of impasto may be equated with the composite character of the fabric, and suggest the successive contributions of numerous generations to the cathedral, begun in 1150 and completed only in 1509.

CHAPTER 1

DURHAM

Perched on a rockface several hundred feet high, surrounded with dense foliage and almost encircled by the River Wear, the cathedral of Durham has a site unlike any other in Europe. Here, as at many English cathedrals, the best has been made of the setting; the trees have been allowed to grow to their full majesty, the river spanned by two dignified bridges and the precincts turfed to form the lawns of College and Palace Green. But this landscaping took place only during the last two or three hundred years; the core itself has scarcely altered since the middle ages. Cathedral, monastery and castle (which since 1832 has housed the University of Durham) still reflect the formidable combination of temporal and spiritual power that has always held this small peninsula.

The main outline of the building consists of an arrangement of rectangular boxes set either vertically or horizontally at right angles to the longitudinal axis of the main vessel, which is also rectangular and long in the characteristic Anglo-Norman manner. The eastern transept, an Early English addition, repeats this form. All further additions are only embellishments. The first of these is the Joseph Window with intersecting tracery at the north end of the eastern transept; next are the Decorated choir aisle windows, and then the three large Perpendicular windows of the main transept and the west end. All are largely rectilinear in form, blending with the design of the arcading both at ground level and on the upper storeys of the western towers and echoing the rectangular volumes of the main body. Only the traceried heads of these windows and the ogee arches terminating in crocketed finials on the central tower introduce a new note, which softens and enriches the starkness of the Norman forms and harmonises with the natural tracery of the trees below.

Towering majestically over the River Wear is the stronghold formed by the cathedral, monastery and castle of Durham. At the heart of this complex was the precious shrine of St Cuthbert.

Further mellowness is provided by the weathered texture of the ochre sandstone, which is curiously striped in places.

The final addition, the central tower, which was built in two stages —the lower in 1460 and the upper (significantly free of pinnacles) in a different stone in 1490—continues to emphasise the earlier Anglo-Norman concept. The central tower was probably not intended by the Anglo-Norman builders to dominate the composition; it was the role of the western towers to present the appearance of an impregnable fortress. The central tower of Durham stems from a line of magnificent English tower design, dating from that of old St Paul's (begun in 1200); York (1407) and Canterbury (1490) are later examples, which show how the standard of design in no way declined with the waning of the middle ages.

Though stable and foursquare, Durham has several features that

Above, the Neville Screen (1372–80), designed to provide niches for alabaster images. Executed with machine-like precision, it comprises five four-storeyed octagonal spires alternating with four three-storeyed square ones set diagonally.

Far left, the massive piers and bold ribbed vaulting (one of the earliest surviving examples) have extraordinary power and vitality. Note the surprisingly successful addition of the exuberant font cover.

Left, a stole of silk and gold thread (c. 910), presented to St Cuthbert's shrine, reflects King Alfred's encouragement of Anglo-Saxon art along classical lines at the time. 31

combine to add a vertical lift to the composition. First, of course, are the pointed arches of the Gothic windows, and it is worth noticing how in the upper stages of the west towers, tall pointed arches alternate with squat, semicircular ones, thus still combining the vertical and horizontal elements. In addition, the towers become more open in the upper storeys. In the 14th century, lead-covered wooden spires were added to the two towers of the west end; these survived until the Commonwealth. A stone spire was even planned in the early 16th century, and the 18th-century architect James Wyatt (who carried out so many 'improvements' in the interior) planned a further spire in 1795. The termination to the towers intended by the Normans was pyramidal, similar to the restored spires at Southwell. Significantly Durham today has none of these tentative spires and is marked by an extraordinary unity of style found in no other English cathedral except Salisbury and Exeter.

Inside the same unity prevails. The cylindrical piers are of cyclopean size, yet their massiveness is enlivened by bold geometrical patterns. Alternating with them are compound piers, whose shafts rise without interruption and curve finally into the vaults. The feeling created, however, is still very unGothic. The idea of a wall is still strongly suggested by the cylindrical piers spaced at intervals of no more than seven feet (the size of their diameter) and by the compound piers some ten feet across. Another important contribution to this initial impression is made by two groups of furnishing.

The first to be seen are several pieces of handsome Restoration woodwork, which were made under the direction of John Cosin, bishop between 1662 and his death in 1672. These, though the only example of furnishing of this period to be found in a cathedral, are even more interesting for their curious combination of medieval and Carolean motifs. One of them, the font cover, 40 feet high and 9 feet across, is a rich and splendid piece well-foiled by its sturdy Norman surroundings. There is further work in the choir—a prayer desk, a complete set of stalls, screens for the choir aisles, and parclose screens to these aisles. Among Baroque scrolls and cherubs' heads, these screens incorporate tracery that is so close to Perpendicular work that it could be classed as a remarkably early instance of a deliberate Gothic revival, in contrast to the tail-end 'survival' look of the font and stalls.

Another and even more important item of furnishing is the sedilia and altar screen given by John Neville in 1380. Carved out of stone from Caen, it was shipped in boxes from London to Sunderland,

In the plan, below, note the double transepts (the eastern contains the Chapel of the Nine Altars) and at the west end, the Galilee or Lady Chapel.

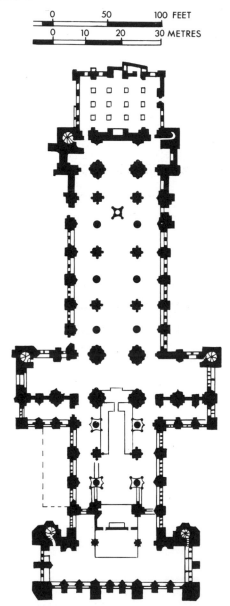

A view across the nave. Power and vitality are the keynotes of this design with its lofty arcade, strong alternation of piers, blind wall arcading and bold geometrical patterning.

The intriguing vault of the monks' kitchen (1366–71) comprises an octagonal louvre projected to form a stellar vault—a close copy of Islamic design.

33

The Galilee Chapel (c. 1170–5), built in the final phase of the Anglo-Norman style; its five parallel aisles and repetitive decoration give it an accidental resemblance to a mosque.

reassembled and provided with 107 painted and gilded alabaster images. All that remains today is the framework, but the machine-like precision of its slim vertical forms, some set square and some canted, has the refinement and sophistication of a design by Mies van der Rohe.

The history of the cathedral can be said to begin in 995. In this year, the monks of Lindisfarne, who had been compelled by Viking raids to seek safety inland, built the 'White Church' on the site of the present cathedral. In this church, the monks deposited the coffin containing the bones of St Cuthbert, who had become bishop of Lindisfarne in 685. Northumbria at the time of Cuthbert was the

most powerful kingdom of Britain and probably in this dark age

Above, part of the large traceried window (1280–90), the earliest of several at Durham at the north end of the Chapel of the Nine Altars. The clean intersecting lines enriched with foiled circles and a second layer of tracery initiated a new, uniquely English development in window design.

Left, the Chapel of the Nine Altars (c. 1242–80), built as a dignified setting for St Cuthbert's shrine, is a powerful composition of slender lancets arranged in threes, their vertical lines accentuated by alternate shafting in sandstone and grey marble and stabilised by the central rose (a restoration of Wyatt).

35

the most civilised corner of Western Europe. Not only were there many monasteries, notably the famous libraries of Wearmouth and Jarrow, but a high standard of design and craftsmanship in the arts, as can be seen in the Northumbrian crosses of Ruthwell and Bewcastle (which are still *in situ*) and in such illuminated manuscripts as the Book of Durrow and the Lindisfarne Gospels.

The present cathedral was begun by Bishop William de St Carilef, who laid the foundation stone of the choir in August 1093. (Although no fire or other calamity damaged the earlier Saxon church, not a trace of it is visible.) By 1104 the choir was vaulted, and by 1128 the transepts and nave were finished. The vaults of the nave were completed five years later; the whole enterprise therefore lasted no more than 40 years. Work was then immediately begun on the chapter house (which was finished by 1140)—an apsed and vaulted rectangular building enriched with interlaced arcading and zigzag decoration similar to that of the later parts of the nave. After the chapter house, the final work in the Norman style was the Galilee Chapel, built around 1170–5 by Bishop Pudsey. The next project was the extension of the choir, which was built between 1242 and 1280 in the new Gothic style. This constituted a second transept, which was intended to provide a more dignified setting for St Cuthbert's shrine and at the same time accommodation for nine more altars. Apart from three large windows—those in the west end (*c.* 1341), the north transept (1345–81) and south transept (*c.* 1420–90)—the central tower and the cloisters, no further building was carried out during the Decorated and Perpendicular periods either in the cathedral nor to any extent in the county at large.

What were the innovations made at Durham? Proportions in the elevation look forward to the vertical emphasis of Gothic. At Ely and Peterborough, arcade, gallery and clerestory are more-or-less equal in proportion; at Durham, the arcade is just less than two-thirds of the total height, so that the gallery looks almost like a triforium and the clerestory seems to be enveloped by the vaults, which themselves continue this upward movement. The whole design, indeed, has a new boldness, which is also seen in the more staccato effect of the alternating compound and cylindrical piers, in the more pronounced projection of the vaulting shafts and finally in the decoration.

Here, for the first time, stimulating geometrical patterns are used on a large scale not only in paint but incised into the stone, first in the form of the spiral grooving of the piers in the choir, then of a

All the power and magnificence of Durham are revealed in this view of the bold, vaulted Anglo-Norman choir, embellished by later generations with the elegant Neville Screen, the combined tomb, altar and throne of Bishop Hatfield (restored to its original rich colours) and the unusual early Restoration choir stalls.

zigzag in the transepts; finally, in the nave, a diaper pattern and fluting are added. This strength and splendour is further enriched by a smaller zigzag, which decorates the orders of the arches and vaulting ribs in the nave between the first and second bays, and continues as the work proceeds westwards. In addition, the west portal (now filled in by the east wall of the Galilee Chapel), the north portal and the south-west portal (which lead to the cloisters) incorporate foliage and animals, and the chapter house, caryatid figures. This tendency towards greater luxury is evident throughout the country at this time, and at Durham reached its climax in the Galilee Chapel.

The Galilee Chapel was originally intended as a Lady Chapel, and was in fact started as an extension to the original apsed east end. It had to be destroyed, however, because St Cuthbert, according to legend, would have no women worshipping near his bones. In fact, there is a line of grey Frosterly marble in the pavement of the nave (which lies as far back as the font) beyond which women were not allowed to trespass. The decoration of the Galilee Chapel combines all the richness of late Norman work in the cathedral with a lightness and airiness found in Early Gothic work of this time. Its design recalls that of a Cluniac antechamber and its waterleaf capitals are those used by the Cistercians. In the jambs of the arched recess to the north of the original portal are portraits of St Oswald and St Cuthbert, which are rare examples of paintings surviving from this period.

At the other end of the cathedral is another chapel, that of the Nine Altars. Though not so secluded, it is next door to the tomb of St Cuthbert and has a design of greater distinction. Partly financed by an indulgence announced as early as 1235, the chapel is in the form of a second transept (the site prevented any further building to the east)—a form that has an antecedent in Fountains but no successors. Since it was aisleless, it had few architectural possibilities. It is the only part of the cathedral within partial view from the nave not in the Anglo-Norman style, although the bold mass of shafts that make up the central buttresses and deeply set trios of lancet windows have a similar dignity and strength. Only the arcading below is cramped and poor. The floor here is almost six feet lower, presumably to give an illusion of height and verticality. A special pleasure is the Joseph Window at the north end—a pattern of trefoiled and cinquefoiled circles set in intersecting tracery, all of which is repeated in a second layer. The design is inspired by the Angel Window at Lincoln, also the home of the style of sculpture exemplified
38 in the beautiful central boss of the four evangelists. This ties together

The ribbed vault from the choir aisle, above, is probably the earliest in existence; it dates from 1095–1100.

Right, the sanctuary knocker of Durham (1100–25), a rare example of its time. Even without its original enamel eyes, it illustrates the power of Romanesque imagery.

the ribs of the complex vaults that join the trapezoid bays of the chapel on to the choir aisles.

Vaulting is a speciality of Durham. The choir aisles are agreed by most to have been finished by 1096. They are therefore the earliest surviving ribbed vaults in Europe (although controversially dated competitors for the title exist in North Italy). Previously only apses, aisles, narrow aisleless naves or crypts had been tunnel-vaulted or groin-vaulted. The first major nave vaults are tunnel vaults, and appeared in France in the 1070s, while the first example of a groin-vaulted nave was built at Speier in the 1080s. By this period there was an increasing enthusiasm for vaulting churches. Its advantages were several; it was both more practical and more aesthetic than the open rafters or timber ceiling previously used, since it was less susceptible to fire and united walls and ceiling in a single material. It also presented a challenge to the builders. The peculiarity of Durham is that its vaulting was by means of ribs with developed mouldings that continue the articulation of the structure below. Strangely there were no immediate successors in England; the ribbed vault first reappears in Normandy—and then only in the 1120s—from where it later spread to the Ile de France.

Nevertheless, Durham had its teething troubles. The choir was undoubtedly meant to be vaulted from the beginning, because of the presence of two demi-shafts that rise from the cill of the gallery on either side of the three main shafts of the compound pier. These demi-shafts could only be there to support the diagonal ribs. But by the 13th century, the main vault was full of cracks and the present vault is a replacement of this time. In the transepts too are discrepancies and signs of hesitation. As for the vaulting of the nave, which was not finished until 1133, it appears to be an afterthought since the supporting corbels were only cut out of the walls at the springing of the arches of the vault. Several interesting developments can be observed. The bays in the nave are oblong in the High Gothic style, instead of square as in the choir; the transverse arches appear only at every other bay and are pointed; the cells of the vaults towards the west are 12–6 inches thick, compared with the 20 inches of the earlier ones; and the galleries that withstand the outward thrust of the vaults are now supplied internally with quadrant arches instead of the semicircular ones found in the choir—in short, an internal flying buttress. This final achievement makes Durham one of the outstanding creations of the middle ages; the principle of its design was followed until the building of Notre Dame at Paris began in 1163.

CHAPTER 2

LAON

At the summit of a hill so steep that direct ascent can only be made by steps or funicular is the commanding silhouette of the cathedral of Laon. Halfway up the hill on which the cathedral stands there are considerable stretches of the old fortified walls; near the top the streets become narrow, reaching to within a few yards of the cathedral and the bishop's palace. Only the façade has a small empty square in front of it. And how effective is this sudden encounter.

Facing the west front, our eyes first enter the deep rounded recesses of the porches, then jump to the intervening tabernacles, up their pinnacles to the next storey with its heavily moulded windows. Our glance then leaps to the arcaded gallery, which also seems to jump by way of more pinnacled tabernacles to the octagonal towers apparently gyrating to their summits. The centrally placed rose window gives the design a certain equilibrium, but its revolving form also adds movement. Other towers over the transepts, again octagonal and open to the elements, also participate in this barbaric rhythmic dance that crowns the capital city of Aisne, once a capital of the Carolingian kings.

Stormy episodes mark the history of Laon and its cathedral. The earliest record tells how on April 25, 1112 the citizens rose against the notorious Bishop Gaudri, who had annulled their charter and set fire to the treasury of the chapter. The fire reached the cathedral, where it gained such a hold that it destroyed the timbers of the roof, melted the gold plaques of the altar and various reliquaries and shrines. This earlier cathedral, however, cannot have been completely gutted, since we learn that services were resumed a few days later.

Further accounts relate how the new bishop, Barthélemy de Jur,

A view of the central crossing of Laon looking towards the north transept. The opening up of the walls through four storeys and the dynamic soar of the main piers create a grid of canalised energy in quite a modern idiom.

41

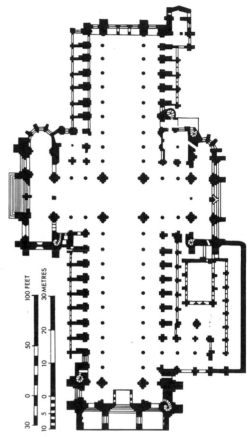

and the canons set about collecting funds. After less than three months, seven canons accompanied by a few laymen started to tour from town to town exhibiting the most precious items from their treasury and asking for offerings. In the spring of 1113 another mission set out for England and returned seven months later with enough money to restore the cathedral in time for it to be consecrated the following year.

Only half a century later, funds were being solicited again, this time for the total rebuilding of the cathedral, the reason for which is uncertain. Bishop Gauthier de Montagne inaugurated the first campaign for the new building (the cathedral we know today), which began about 1160. This comprised a sanctuary of only three 42 compartments or bays, an apse, and the eastern bays of the transept,

Above, a plan of the cathedral. Note the unusual (for France) length of the choir—an early 13th-century replacement of the original choir of only three bays with apse and ambulatory.

Above left, the bold and defiant silhouette of the cathedral on its hilltop site—an image that aptly reflects the stormy history of Laon.

Right, the west front of Laon (1190–1225) is characterised by a sense of energy and a bold use of relief in its gable porches, rose window and open towers—all new and important features in the development of the Gothic style.

43

which also terminated in apses. The second campaign, begun in 1180, finished the transepts, put up the nave and by 1230 completed the western façade and the towers. At the same time the choir (which presumably had collapsed) was rebuilt and lengthened by seven bays. Later, side chapels were added and the south transept windows altered, but basically the cathedral is the conception of the last two generations of the 12th century.

The resulting unity of design is especially remarkable in the light and cheerful interior. Throughout its unusual length runs a four-storey elevation, which, when compared with that of Durham built two generations earlier, is both more lofty, more articulated and more alert. At Durham the massive piers almost lumber towards the altar, whereas the slim columns at Laon flow more quickly in their rhythm. This is largely the result of the scarcely noticeable difference in the design of the bays—the variation from three to five in the number of vaulting shafts and from octagonal to square in the shape of the bases and abaci of the main piers, though in the later choir even these are identical. This feeling of alertness is also created by a greater elimination of the wall, which gives the interior the new

The Renaissance screens (1572–5), left, with their haphazard compilation of classical motifs, are handsomely foiled by their sturdy setting.

Right, a view showing the pronounced transepts and lantern crossing, which, with the long choir, give the cathedral an English feeling. Note the combination of round and pointed arches.

44

lightness and transparency of the Gothic style. Indeed, Laon is as perfect an embodiment of the Early Gothic as Durham is of the Anglo-Norman.

Like all medieval buildings, Laon combines inherited ideas and new developments or experiments. The capacious galleries are Norman in origin and were probably not intended for pilgrims, since the spiral staircases of the fabric were too slight to have withstood the passage of large crowds. Here the galleries were meant to sustain the outward thrust of the stone vaults and to carry their weight down on to the aisle walls and from there to the ground. Nor is the triforium a new feature, since it is found in Burgundian Romanesque. Here it is hollowed out of the walls and provides access to remote parts of the building for maintenance and ventilation. Originally it made an entire circuit of the building, running the length of the main vessels and transepts, threading its way along the exterior in the transept apses (as in other churches of the Champagne district) and emerging again on the outside of the west front, where it linked up to staircases in the towers. There are other links, of which the most remarkable is that with four spiral staircases hollowed out of the main crossing piers. These stairs lead up to the arcaded gallery of the lantern tower and from there to the rafters. Similarly, a blind arcade originally encircled the entire interior of the aisle walls at ground level. The vaults again derive from Anglo-Norman designs of the early 12th century in which each unit or bay is divided into six compartments. This sexpartite design continued to be used until Chartres.

A more recently developed feature is the combination of both gallery and triforium into a four-storey elevation. This had appeared a decade earlier at Noyon and in the choir of St Remi at Reims, but may have originated even earlier in churches in the neighbourhood of Tournai. The even articulation is of course Romanesque in character, but at Laon the wall is almost replaced by a structure in relief so that space begins to flow from area to area in a manner that is essentially Gothic. This quality of relief is also an outstanding characteristic of the façade. Another recent—perhaps even original—development at Laon is the wall-buttress, a wedge of masonry filling the area between the gallery vaults and their roofs and pierced with doorways for circulation. Curiously, when the choir was rebuilt in 1220, the wall-buttress system of the nave was repeated in identical form.

46   The square termination of the choir is unusual in France. The

Above, the light and youthful interior of Laon. Shafts shoot from capitals to vaults and four storeys enliven the walls. Only the cylindrical piers and the individual units of the windows are unintegrated, giving Laon an early Gothic look.

Right, a view showing one of the transept chapels (c. 1160–80), the most advanced feature of the building. Its polygonal form, bold buttressing and almost total elimination of the wall look forward to the lantern of glass of High Gothic.

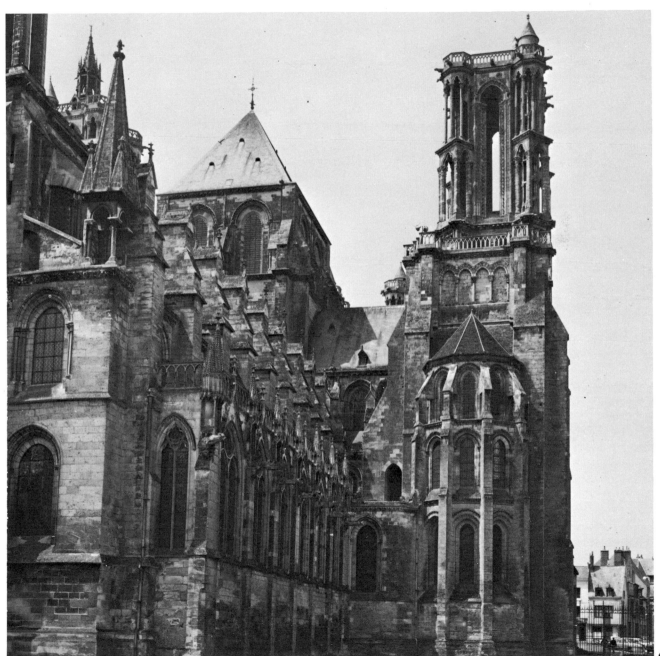

47

explanation was probably the previous unsuccessful semicircular design of the apse and the ambulatory scaled up to a height of four storeys and the resulting difficulties in vaulting. The square end was easy to achieve and at least matched the transepts. On the other hand, the addition of seven extra bays on to the earlier remaining three is more difficult to justify.

The design of the transept apses is quite new and of far-reaching significance. They are polygonal—a form that is found in the apses of the two chapels in the near-by bishop's palace built by Bishop Gauthier a decade before the cathedral was begun. The original choir apse was also polygonal, and is the earliest example of this form (which was to become such a popular feature of the High Gothic style) since early Christian times. Viewed from any angle, a

Above, the voussoirs and tympanum of the left-hand portal, dedicated to the Virgin. The third and fourth voussoirs depict episodes from the Old Testament prefiguring the Virgin Birth, interpreted to the masons by clerics from Laon's famous cathedral school.

Right, a detail from a prefiguration of the Virgin Birth from the left-hand portal. It shows the prophet Habbakuk transported from Judea by an angel and carrying a basket of food, which he passed into Daniel's den without breaking the king's seal.

48

polygonal apse will always provide a series of multiple images whereas a semicircular apse can only be viewed satisfactorily from one point. Even more significant, the growing popularity of stained glass at the turn of the 12th and 13th centuries was more easily accommodated in a window that was flat than in one that was curved.

The detail too is worth mentioning, for its minor variations in design show the essentially empirical approach that is responsible for the living quality of medieval buildings. An obvious example of early experiments in design is the domed effect of the aisle vaulting in the bays of the choir nearest the south transept. Another is the addition of monolithic colonettes to the second and fourth piers of the nave nearest the crossing. This design anticipates the shafted pier of the High Gothic style. The capitals are far from uniform. The earliest, in the eastern aisles of the transepts, are carved with acanthus leaves and other rich stylised foliage, often with scrolls inhabited by men or beasts. Later capitals in the nave are decorated with local vegetation—celandine, watercress, plantain, buttercup, and in the choir the foliage is crocketed. Similarly, the profiles of the mouldings vary from early simple roll mouldings to combinations of increasing elaboration and sophistication.

At one time the cathedral blazed with two thousand stained-glass windows, of which only the rose of the north transept and the four windows of the choir remain. The most interesting of these is the left-hand lancet in the choir, which tells the story of the modest vassal Theophilus who sold his soul to Satan in return for the chance to become a bishop—an offer he had previously refused. Once he had succeeded, he was overcome by remorse and knelt in prayer in front of a statue of the Virgin, who appeared and returned his pact. He thereupon made a public confession of his crime. Of all the many miracles attributed to the Virgin, this story was paid particular attention by the Church, who appreciated the universal appeal of its Faustian theme. In the rose window of the north transept are represented the seven liberal arts first outlined by St Augustine. (These were divided into the Trivium or the arts of speech—grammar, rhetoric and dialectic—and the Quadrivium or the arts of mathematics—arithmetic, geometry, astronomy and music.) The mother of these was philosophy and together they comprised all the wordly knowledge accessible to medieval man. The liberal arts are depicted only at Chartres and at Laon, whose cathedral school attracted students from Germany and Italy for half a century.

To emphasise the accent on learning, the liberal arts are repeated

(with the addition of philosophy, architecture and medicine) on the west front round the windows to the left of the rose. (The companion window on the right of the rose shows the scenes of the Creation.) But one of the outstanding examples of medieval scholarship appears in the left portal of the west front, which, like the centre portal, is dedicated to the Virgin Mary. It sets out in the two outer voussoirs a series of episodes from the Old Testament prefiguring the Virgin Birth, which is unparalleled in its range and ingenuity. For instance, there is the story of Gideon, the judge of Israel who spread a fleece on a threshing floor which, when the dew descended, remained dry. In the innermost band is a series of adoring angels with a symbol of the Holy Ghost on the keystone and on the next band the virtues overcoming the vices. (The Virgin was said by the Doctors of the Church to possess all the virtues.) The life-size standing figures (which are modern) and the lintel relate the cardinal events in the Virgin's life: the Presentation, Annunciation, Visitation and Nativity. Finally in the central panel or tympanum is represented the climax to this eulogy: the Adoration of the Three Wise Men. The much earlier Romanesque right-hand portal is devoted to the Last Judgement, unusual for the time since the inspiration comes from the gentler account of St Matthew rather than the usual version of St John. As in the centre portal, the jamb figures are 19th-century replicas from Chartres. Laon suffered severely during the Revolution, and there is much obvious restoration. Even so, one can still appreciate the significance of the new, elaborate schemes for the portal sculpture, which were to become such an important feature shortly afterwards at Paris, Chartres, Amiens and Reims.

The architecture was even more influential; the west front created the prototype that was imitated throughout the 13th century. It occurs in the north and south façades at Chartres, in the west front at Reims, Strasbourg and Halberstadt. Another essential feature of the Gothic style is the skyline, which at Laon includes the fullest complement of towers of any cathedral of the middle ages. The model was Tournai, built in the mid-12th century, where the towers are square in plan and their only decoration is rows of arcading. Impressively menacing as they are, they are dull by the side of the octagonal forms and relief silhouette of the towers of Laon. This design was a totally new conception for the neighbourhood, and it influenced numerous cathedrals on the other side of the Rhine— Bamberg, Naumberg, Freiburg, Limburg, Halberstadt, all of which 50 reflect various aspects of Laon.

Above, an Old Testament prophecy of the birth of Christ represented on the left-hand portal: Balaam on the mountain of Peor tells the people of Israel that a star shall be born of Jacob.

The relief silhouette and sense of movement in the remarkable towers of Laon (right) are already essentially Gothic. The carved oxen at their summits commemorate those that hauled the cartloads of stone.

51

cathedral of this capital city rather than a cathedral with royal associations. It was, however, connected with the university, which grew out of the cathedral school. The square in front was the campus, and bookstalls were set up in front of the cathedral; it was also used as a stage by lay players and the famous minstrels of Notre Dame.

Notre Dame was begun in 1163 and the choir and the eastern bays of the transepts were finished in 19 years. The western bays and the adjacent bays of the nave followed immediately, and by 1225 the cathedral was complete up to but not including the upper gallery of the west front. During the next 25 years, until 1250, the towers and the High Gothic additions were completed. These included the enlargement of the upper windows and the addition of elementary bar tracery, the resulting reinforcement with giant buttresses and the

insertion of aisle chapels into the spaces between the original

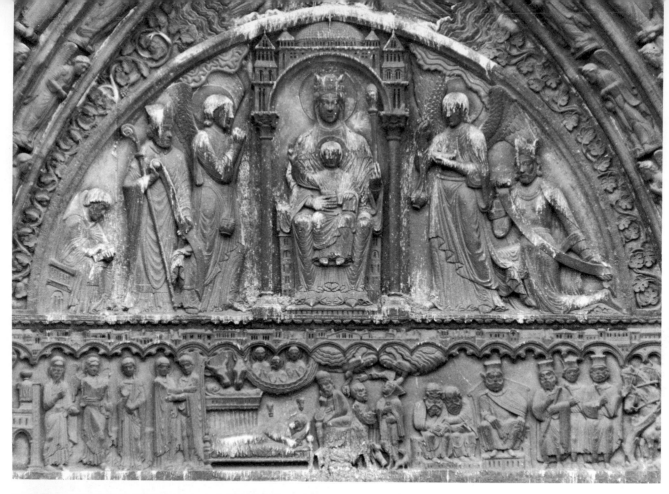

Above, the tympanum of the St Anne portal of the west front, dating from the 1160s, depicting the dedication of Notre Dame to the Virgin by the founder, Maurice de Sully, and King Louis VII. Note the manuscript-derived technique and the canopies of miniature towns.

Left, four of eight reliefs from the piers of St Stephen's portal (c. 1260), thought to represent scenes from student life. The fluid handling of the figures and the genre incidents in the corners give them a fresh charm of their own.

56

buttresses. This extension of the building line meant that the transepts were reduced by one bay at their junction with the nave, so to reassert their importance, new transept façades were designed. Later additions were only minor. These included a triple chapel at the head of the chancel built between 1280 and 1296, other chapels on either side, which continued until 1330, and finally the pinnacles and finials between 1333–8 by the master-mason Jean Ravy.

Notre Dame and the cathedral of Laon are contemporaries and there is considerable similarity in their interiors. Both have cylindrical piers and sexpartite vaulting. Like Laon, Notre Dame originally had a four-storey elevation of which the third storey was in the form of small rose windows or oculi. (This design was reintroduced by Viollet-le-Duc in the bays next to the crossing.) The major difference between the two is the design of the bays, which at Paris are uniform with only three vaulting shafts repeated the length of the cathedral, and above all, the added 30 feet in height. As a result, the interior moves in a quicker rhythm towards the altar and has an elevation that almost soars. The absence of obvious variation in detail and the reduction of the elevation to three storeys adds a quality of simple nobility. Similarly, the plan is one spatial unit compared with the collection of juxtaposed units at Laon. The five aisles on the other hand and the wealth of vistas provided by the double side aisles as they encircle the choir add a sense of richness. Another almost hidden richness appears in the inner aisles where every other intermediary pier is surrounded by shafts of colonnettes.

Two criticisms have been levelled at the cathedral at Paris. The first is the darkness of the interior, which is particularly striking when recalling Laon. This sombre effect is not only attributable to the absorption of light by the glass, but is mainly produced by the doubled-aisled design. The twice-repeated sloping roofs, first of the outer aisles and then of the inner galleries, restricted the area of wall available for windows and also forced the position of the gallery upwards, so that light from these was just adequate for the gallery. Above, the clerestory windows were pushed up into the vaults. The improvement in lighting made possible by the introduction of exposed flying buttresses and enlarged windows was partly counteracted by the extra width added by the aisle chapels. The second unsatisfactory feature is the rounded as opposed to polygonal apse. In the earlier small windows, the curved surfaces of the stained glass would have been scarcely noticeable, but they are much more apparent in the enlarged windows introduced in 1230.

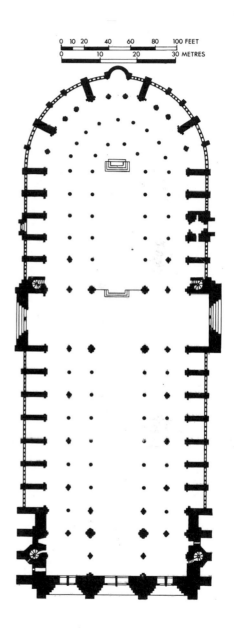

Concentration and centralisation are the significant features of this plan with its absence of protruding transepts. Its five-aisled design is only found in major ecclesiastical enterprises. 57

The new transept façades were partly designed to solve the problem of darkness. An inscription in Latin at the foot of the south façade tells us that it was begun in 1258, during the lifetime of Jean de Chelles and finished by Pierre de Montereuil—the most famous architect of the second half of the 13th century. They are inspired by those designed by Pierre at St Denis, but are far more audacious. To a height of 59 feet, the walls have been eliminated and replaced by mosaics of glass. Of these, only the rose window of the north transept survives more or less intact. It celebrates the glory of the Virgin, who is acclaimed by 16 prophets, 32 kings of Judah and 32 patriarchs and

The five-aisled plan of Notre Dame (which posed so many problems) is seen, opposite, in all its richness. As well as capacious accommodation, it provided the multiplicity of views so popular at this period.

Left, the south transept façade, with its overall pattern of tracery above the five-gabled portal, is remarkable for the daring elimination of wall.

high priests, all of whom occupy medallions arranged in a series of concentric circles. The south window has been reset at least twice, as has the rose of the west front. (These windows made a great impression on Viollet-le-Duc as a child. In his old age, he recalled how they had reminded him of the huge flowers of a funeral wreath, sad and resplendent, which seemed to break into song when the organ began to play.) The 12 high windows of the nave are filled with glass commissioned from 12 different artists in 1938 and are interesting as early examples of modern glass.

More can be learnt, however, about the new developments appearing in the transepts by looking at their exteriors. The south transept is the later and more evolved of the two, and strikes us first with the overall decoration of its surface, which includes five 'portals',

Personifications of three virtues—Humility, Prudence and Justice—on either side of the central Judgement portal; below them, their corresponding vices are represented by exemplary scenes. Note the plastic treatment of the virtues compared with the inset cameos and negative columns of the vices.

Gravity and tenderness characterise the tympanum (c. 1210), above, of the left-hand portal of the west front, where traces of the original gilding still exist on the figure of Mary.

Left, part of the beautifully composed tympanum of the north transept (c. 1250), also dedicated to the Virgin. Here, above scenes of Christ's infancy, is related the miracle of the cleric Theophilus, whom Mary delivered from his pact with the Devil.

61

four of which are blind (like the pair on the main façade of Reims). Further study reveals a new turn in the evolution of forms—a desire to blend the two favourite geometrical motifs of the Early Gothic designers, the circle and the pointed arch. In the west front there is a juxtaposition and balancing of these forms, but on the south façade some of the circular forms become pointed; these rounded triangles form the first circle next to the two roses.

To return to the west front, which seems so flat after Laon, but whose simple majesty and coherence of design is revealed on a second viewing. The gallery of kings connects both the vertical and horizontal elements; similarly the upper gallery joins the body of the cathedral to the tower, acting, it has been said, like 'a pair of lace cuffs'. The small discrepancies add life to the design—the left portal with its lower arches, the extra breadth of the left tower, on which one can count eight kings as opposed to only seven on the right-hand side. But these are small details compared with the portals, in which the whole philosophy of the age is displayed.

In the centre is the Last Judgement. The grandest treatment of this theme appears at Bourges, but at Paris for the first time the humanity of St Matthew's account finds new forms. (The archaic tympanum at Laon did no more than illustrate the text.) The most impressive figure is that of the Judging Christ, full of majesty and compassion, while eager angels perch precariously in the voussoir above. Below are scenes of the Resurrection, the separation of the Blessed and the Damned and, on the jambs, the apostles (all restorations of Viollet-le-Duc). Finally, there are the 12 virtues, placed inescapably at eye-level above their corresponding vices. An interesting relic from the Romanesque treatment of this subject appears in the lowest voussoirs, on the right of which the Riders of the Apocalypse are depicted as reminders of the reign of terror that will accompany the coming of the Son of Man.

Both the left- and right-hand portals are dedicated to the Virgin, whose glorification is the subject of four of the six portals, a series of quatrefoil reliefs on the north façade and of two of the rose windows. Her cult had been increasing since the 12th century, largely because of the influence of St Bernard, who sang her praises in his sermons and in his commentary on the *Song of Songs*. In her cathedral at Paris the Queen of Heaven is presented first of all in the early Portail St Anne, where she is seated under a canopy, a figure of terrifying and uncanny aloofness. This tympanum was probably carved shortly after building was started on the choir, and was

Above, the proud figure of Mary—the only genuinely medieval jamb figure at Paris—stands on the centre doorpost of the north transept under a capital of fresh young foliage.

Attention was lavished even on the more remote parts of a medieval cathedral, as can be seen in the view, left, of the budding crockets and the famous gargoyles (recreated by Viollet-le-Duc). 63

considered of such importance that it was incorporated into an enlarged portal 40 to 50 years later; extra figures were added to left and to right and another band recording the life of St Anne on to the bottom of the lintel.

The Virgin next appears on the left-hand portal, in representations of her death and resurrection (combined for the first time in one scene) and of her coronation. This subject had been treated before at Senlis and at Chartres, but here it is represented with a simple majesty that recalls early Greek sculpture. The scene depicting the occupations of the various months and the corresponding signs of the Zodiac on the plinths below show the same grave economy of style; July sharpening his scythe is a particularly fine example.

The Coronation of the Virgin, some fifty years later in date, appears on the tympanum of the little Porte Rouge on the north façade, but here the royal couple, St Louis and his wife, have been admitted and the tone is intimate and almost conversational. Above, in the voussoirs, appear stories from the life of the local saint Marcel; between are arches of wild briar. Near by is the portal of the north transept, on which appears the story (already encountered at Laon) of the Virgin and the scholar Theophilus, who sold his soul to the Devil and on the lintel, episodes in the life of Mary. The action of the groups, balanced by the intervening empty spaces, recalls the solemn drama of a Giotto fresco and makes it one of the most beautiful tympana of this period.

Mary's life is told once more in the early 14th-century quatrefoils on the plinths of the north apsidal chapels. The change in style is remarkable. The sculpture is expressionistic, even hysterical, and no longer integrated with the architecture but merely set into the wall. There is also a search for new subjects, which include the story from *The Golden Legend* about the Funeral of the Virgin: the High Priest of the Jews, on trying to knock down the coffin, found his hands withering and cleaving to the bier. The whole tenor of these reliefs anticipates the more emotional and pietistic attitudes of the later middle ages.

To find sculpture more suited to the character of Notre Dame, we must return to the portal of the north transept. Here, on the central post dividing the doorway, is a statue of the Virgin, the only standing figure at Notre Dame to survive from the middle ages. She may lack a sense of mystery, yet her air of simple nobility is related to the monumental quality of the cathedral itself, apparent in its five-aisled plan, in its great height and above all in its west front.

The unique character of Notre Dame, seen here from the River Seine, derives from the combination of two distinct styles. The hulk is Early Gothic (c. 1163–1200), over which were superimposed from 1200 onwards High Gothic flying buttresses, pierced stonework, window tracery, and finally the spire.

CHAPTER 4

BOURGES

Far right, the gaunt ruined ugly, yet supremely impressive, west front rises like the conscience of Bourges above the limited everyday world of the city.

Below, one of the most remarkable interiors ever built. The five-aisled design with the stepped elevation of its arcades and its lack of transepts has an unusual unity, combining breadth with height.

The most impressive approach to the cathedral of Bourges is by way of the narrow cobbled streets that lead up to the amazingly broad façade—the five capacious porches and six stout buttresses set across a generous platform of steps. Higher up, the design at first has a jumbled appearance: four storeys of simple Early Gothic windows on the south tower and, on the north tower, the delicate filigree and crocketing of the Flamboyant style. In addition, there are elliptical arches, a newel staircase and on the topmost platform, a gazebo, all features reminiscent of a Renaissance château. In between is the big west window, whose 14th-century tracery blends the rectangular and arched forms of the façade; its culminating feature is the pointed circle of its magnificent rose. Yet despite this mixture of styles—and, in addition, the scars inflicted by the iconoclasts of the religious wars—the façade smoulders with majesty and grandeur.

Inside, the lightness and unity of style could hardly be in greater contrast. The forms are youthful, resilient and uncluttered. The only characteristic in common with the exterior is the sense of breadth. As well as the west–east axis and the view of the double aisles as they encircle the choir, there is the lateral axis common to each bay, where the elevations of the nave and double aisles present a further vista of overlapping layers. On the ground storey are the outer-aisle windows, above which are the triforium and clerestory windows of the inner aisle and, on top of an unbelievably high arcade, the triforium and clerestory windows of the nave. Over and above this abundance of vistas is the enclosing shell of the vaults and roofs, which are of an unprecedented height of 125 feet compared with a breadth of 134 feet. Bourges is all interior, and its unity of space recalls the exhibition halls of glass and iron of the 19th century.

Considerable traces of earlier fabrics can still be found in the cathedral. Deep in the bowels of the crypt below the second and third bays of the choir is a ninth-century Carolingian building, which runs, curiously, at right angles to that of the cathedral. Off the central bay a narrowing gangway leads off to a Treasury building, which may date back to the fifth century. From the Romanesque cathedral (probably built in the second quarter of the 12th century) there survive the two handsome portals of the north and south sides. In the choir of this building Louis VII was twice crowned king of France on two Christmas Days, in 1137 and 1145.

The present cathedral is the result of the efforts of Archbishop Henry de Sully, brother of Eudes de Sully, who completed Notre

Dame in Paris. In 1195, Henry de Sully donated a large sum of money for repairs, to which he added penalty money levied from transgressors. Before his death in 1199, it was decided to build a new church and by 1218 the remains of his successor, Bishop Guillaume, had been transferred on his canonisation into the choir of the new building. Minor alterations in the design of the triforium and clerestory seem to indicate that a new campaign was started to build the nave, which was probably finished towards 1265. Later in the century, the two side porches were erected and a curious structure, known as *le pilier butant*, built to reinforce the south tower. Throughout this period the crypt had been under construction and it was only at the end of the century that its west wall was completed. At the end of the 14th century, the big west window was inserted. It was designed by the architect Guy de Dammartin for his patron Jean, Duc de Berri. Finally, during the 15th and 16th centuries, the spaces between the buttresses were converted into chapels and lavishly embellished with stained glass and decorative vaulting by well-to-do bourgeois of the town. In 1465, a university was founded. The cathedral at this time must have been at the height of its glory—resplendent with stained glass, the choir decorated with a carved screen and enclosure and furnished with stalls and tapestries.

From now on the story of the cathedral is a succession of disasters. First, in 1505, the north tower collapsed—an event that was half anticipated, since it had already been partially dismantled, rebuilt and then earmarked for demolition. With the aid of contributions from the king and the population of Bourges, who gave the cost of milk and butter during Lent, it was finally rebuilt by 1540. Then came the wars of religion. On May 27, 1562 Gabriel de Lorges, Comte de Montgomery, entered the town and the customary looting took place. All the furnishings, works of art, tombs and relics, including the shrine of St William, were destroyed and the cathedral only narrowly escaped being blown up.

Bourges was built with the cathedral of Paris in mind. The two archbishop brothers both used double aisles that curve round the choir and sexpartite vaulting. But here the comparison ends. The transepts, which have little emphasis at Paris, are dispensed with altogether at Bourges, as are the galleries. Instead, the inner aisles rise to the unprecedented height of 69 feet—the most original feature of the brilliant design, inspired perhaps by the cathedral of Sens but carried out on a far more daring and imaginative scale. This height solved the problem of light, so scarce at Paris, which streams

The view of the apse, above, shows the bold scale of the four-storeyed elevation comprising crypt, outer aisles, clerestory of the inner aisles and clerestory of the nave. Oriel-like apsidal chapels accentuate the staccato effect. (Their steep conical roofs and the double finials of the buttresses are unfortunate 19th-century additions.)

Opposite, a medallion from the window of the Prodigal Son (c. 1215–20)—the gift of the tanners and a favourite subject for stained glass. It depicts the portioning of the Prodigal's father's goods, his departure from home, and encounter with a courtesan; in the centre the elder brother patiently ploughs the fields. 69

in through the windows in the inner aisles unimpeded by a gallery. The other novel feature of Bourges is provided by the piers. These are identical throughout the nave and aisles and with the minimum of difference in the alternation; for the first time the classical Corinthian column has been forgotten. Instead, the pier carries the structure of the vaults down to ground level, interrupted only by the top member or abacus of the capital.

A feature unnoticeable to the human eye is the gradual widening of the nave towards the choir. In the first bay of the west end, the distance north to south from centre to centre of each bay is 48 feet; by the choir the distance is 50 feet. The corresponding narrowing of the adjacent aisles seems to have been intended to correct the optical illusion that parallel vertical lines converge in the distance. The desired effect was that of a colonnade whose noble rhythm was caught and fulfilled in the round of the apse rather than dissolved into a vanishing point, as was the taste of the Renaissance and after.

Such an interior needs no further decoration. The walls that might have been available are almost cut away. The only element necessary was light. After Chartres, Bourges has the finest collection of windows of any cathedral; it is also remarkable for the extensive period that it covers. The disposition of the subjects is carefully planned. The clerestory window of the choir shows in the centre Christ with John the Baptist at his side; on the north side are the 12 prophets who foretold the coming of the Messiah—savage and impressive figures each with a window to himself. Facing them are the 12 apostles who spread the gospel and founded the Church. Below in the inner aisles, as their successors, are the bishops of Berri, 18 of which were removed in the 18th century to lighten the church. Finally, at eye level in the outer aisles of the ambulatory, are the windows dedicated to preaching and interpreting the scriptures, while those in the apsidal chapels depict the saints.

A visitor walking clockwise around the ambulatory first comes across the window (given by the masons) telling the story of Dives and Lazarus, who appears, clapper in hand, as the patron saint of beggars and lepers. Then comes the story of the discovery of the relics of St Stephen, the patron saint of the cathedral to whom a portal is dedicated on the west front. This is followed by one of the most beautiful windows at Bourges—the Good Samaritan, the gift of the weavers. Next are the Prodigal Son, given by the tanners, and the New Alliance, given by the butchers and *charcutiers*. Bourges abounds in the lives of the saints. In an apsidal chapel is an unusually fanciful window depicting incidents in the life of St John the Divine, not one of which is found in canonical books. Miracles, calamities, parables and conversions follow in relentless succession.

All these windows were made in the 13th century and comprise varying arrangements of circular medallions, which contain small pieces of glass that are dark and predominantly blue. The windows in the crypt (*c.* 1404) are made up of larger pieces of glass, which are also lighter in tone with white, pale blue and pink as the predominant colours. They represent a series of graceful apostles and prophets and were originally in the Sainte Chapelle of Bourges. The windows in the side chapels are later; the finest of these, which can be dated 1448–50, is that of the merchant prince and financier Jacques Coeur in the last chapel on the north side of the choir. It is

Far left, the vast crypt at Bourges—an unusual feature in a Gothic cathedral—built to bridge the town moat. Beautiful 14th-century windows and the tomb of the great 15th-century patron Jean, Duc de Berri, are its only ornament.

Left, one of the 40 weepers that once surrounded the tomb of Jean de Berri. The weepers' heavy drapery is as varied as their individual expressions and gestures.

Below, a plan of Bourges, remarkable for its double aisles and unusual lack of transepts.

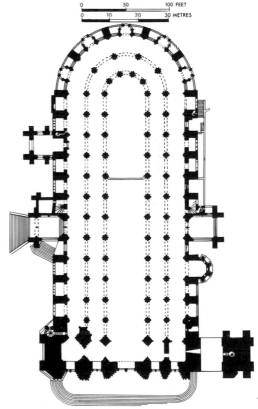

Left, the north portal (c. 1160), a relic of the earlier Romanesque church. The column figures and wild variety of patterns derive from the Portail Royal at Chartres. Note the gorgeous undercut foliage scroll of classical inspiration.

Bourges is remarkable among Gothic cathedrals for its sense of breadth exemplified in the west front, right, by the generous platform of steps, the niched arcading of the splays and the five magnificent portals.

Below, a view of the north porch (c. 1295). The impressive flight of steps and the delicate Moorish decoration make a fine, though curious, foil to the vigorous Romanesque forms behind.

again brilliant in tone, rich in texture and decorated with heraldic insets in the tracery above.

The sculpture of Bourges, though not in the same class as its stained glass, covers an equally long period. The earliest (c. 1160) on the two lateral portals of the 12th-century cathedral, has Romanesque features common to a wide group of churches furnished by the workshop at Chartres. One of these characteristics is the barbaric profusion of abstract and vegetable motifs, the latter largely classical in derivation. The leafy scroll deeply undercut on the lintel of the north portal is a handsome example. The attenuated statues of the jambs, their finely pleated drapery clinging to their columnar figures, are also typical of this school. At the end of the 13th century, porches were added, cubic in form and pierced on three sides with sexfoiled oculi and trilobed semicircular arches. Their decoration is elegant and discreet—tiny vegetable motifs and, on the north porch, diminutive monkeys and owls. The simple geometry of these Moorish forms provide a fine frame for the Romanesque doorway behind, and together they make a remarkable juxtaposition of civilisations.

The west front, despite mutilations, 19th-century restorations and empty niches, is still impressive. An innovation is the arcading, which runs the length of the façade; this was carved between the 13th and 16th centuries with scenes full of a delicate humour and accurate observation from nature. The centre portal of the Last Judgement sets the tone of the whole façade. Below circles of angels and the elect at the apex of the tympanum appear the sun and the moon, beneath which is the figure of Christ—heavy and in the round—his arms raised to show his wounds and attended by angels holding the instruments of his Passion. On his left is the kneeling figure of St John, and on his right, Mary, who intercedes for the world. Below is the separation of souls, presided over by the noble figure of St Michael, the blessed to the bosom of Abraham enthroned in a heavenly mansion and the damned to the mouth of hell, the monster Leviathan in whose jaws a boiling cauldron is tended by prodding devils. These creatures are not only more numerous than their victims but far more grotesque; to show the baseness of their appetites, the sculptor has carved faces on their stomachs. A tendency to caricature also appears in the blessed, whose smiles and postures show self-satisfaction. On the lowest register are the risen dead, who display a remarkable energy and variety of attitude. Below the Resurrection in the corners above the polylobed arches are St Mary Magdalene and St Mary of Egypt, representing repentance; above,

Though mutilated by the Huguenots, this centre portal (1220–95) still evokes the momentous majesty of its theme—the Last Judgement— here unfolded in greater grandeur than in any other cathedral. Note the curious polylobe embellishment to the semicircular arches—a later addition of Moorish inspiration.

on the gable in the corners of the oculus, are the Wise and Foolish Virgins with their lamps exemplifying vigilance.

Thus Bourges is not quite all interior, though the monotony of the transeptless flanks must have impressed the middle ages, for four attempts were made to build a spire. The most ambitious design included a gable constructed at right angles to the main body. Yet even if the exterior can be criticised, the interior is unique for its combination of breadth and height, which was never attempted again in the middle ages. Indeed, Bourges can be compared with one of nature's sports, whose genealogy can be traced but whose offspring are few: only Le Mans and Coutances and a few individual features appearing in several Spanish cathedrals.

Part of the two bottom registers of the Last Judgement, over which St Michael presides with benign nonchalance. The life-like figures are carved nearly in the round and the iron of the scales and the Devil's pitchfork are depicted with an almost 'pop' realism.

The brilliance of this design (left) lies in the unusually lofty arcades of the nave, which thus reveal a wealth of overlapping vistas.

The lack of transepts and central spire results in a certain monotony in this side view (below) of the cathedral.

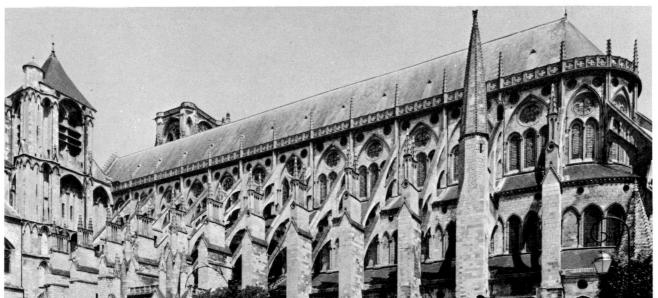

CHAPTER 5

CHARTRES

The stately silhouette of Chartres can be seen from a considerable distance, looming across the cornlands of the Beauce. In the town, it is glimpsed across every bridge and square, mingling with the streets or rising from the ramparts. The town is still small, and the moderate hill on which it is built overlooking the various branches of the River Eure provides the perfect setting.

The hilly site offered dramatic opportunities for silhouetting and may well have inspired, as at Laon, the building of the steeples—an integral part of the medieval image of a cathedral but in France so seldom actually achieved. Originally Chartres was destined to have eight steeples, two on either side of the choir and two on each transept in addition to the two that were in fact built for the west front. Of these, that on the south is one of the greatest architectural achievements of all time. It is best seen from the south-east, from where it acts as a powerful stop to the succession of bold buttresses and flyers leading up to it. The genius of its design lies in the suggestion of upward movement: the strong vertical lines of the lower buttresses and arcading and the increasing height of the storeys gather momentum until, by the third stage, only the sinews of the buttresses are left; the rest is open to the elements. The next storey and the two half-storeys above are the focal point at which energy is gathered for the final leap of the spire. At this stage, the plan changes from square to octagonal by means of dormer windows and gables and the pointed units are superimposed or thickly overlapped like the scales of a growing bud.

The external excrescences of the steeples are also characteristic of the body of the building. The emphasis on the transepts, for example, is striking after the 'liner' silhouette of contemporary Bourges.

Despite the small scale of the portals, the façade of Chartres Cathedral has an extraordinary power and integrity. Even the north steeple contributes to this impression by its greater height and the uncompromising purity of its Flamboyant style; it also adds a note of piquancy.

78

international obligation to contribute to its rebuilding. Money was collected in the usual way—by the sale of indulgences and by attracting business to its four annual fairs, held on the feast days of the Virgin. On the last of these, the Feast of the Nativity, most of the goods sold were religious momentoes, principally *chemisettes*, which when blessed by a priest would help a woman in childbirth or a knight in battle. Funds also came from the distinguished bishop and chapter, who for three years contributed the revenue from what was the largest diocese in France.

From a construction point of view Chartres was a pioneer building. From the start it was provided with flying buttresses, and they are the basic factor of the whole design. Because of them the galleries could be omitted, enabling the clerestory windows to be lengthened and broadened. The master-mason who distilled the principles of his structure to the essentials was also stimulated by the growing taste for stained glass. The glass of this period was dark, so there was an additional incentive for increasing the window area. The clerestory windows were now so large that divisions were necessary—here in the form of a central mullion with a small lobed rose above. Together with the aisle windows below, the cathedral was a fair way to becoming a lantern of glass.

Further developments arise from the design of the clerestory windows. Their semicircular form, occupying the full width and height of each bay, probably encouraged a change in the vaulting system, which is now quadripartite. This gives an even curvature along the length of the vault instead of the uneven 'webbed' interruptions of the earlier sexpartite vaults. The quadripartite system shortened the bays, quickened the rhythm and from Chartres onwards became an established feature of High Gothic. Because of the new method of vaulting, no alternation was necessary in the number of shafts carrying the weight of the vaults down to the piers, for each shaft carried the same load; the alternation was therefore an inherited and purely decorative feature.

For the first time at Chartres, the stained glass and the architecture complement each other. Today it is the abstract beauty of the windows that first strikes us and in the middle ages people marvelled at their resemblance to jewels. The earliest windows at Chartres are the three lancets of the west front, which, with the Portail Royal, escaped the fire of 1194. They are some of the most beautiful glass ever made and are easy to 'read'. The predominating colour is a blue peculiar to the 12th century—a flax blue lighter than those of the 13th century

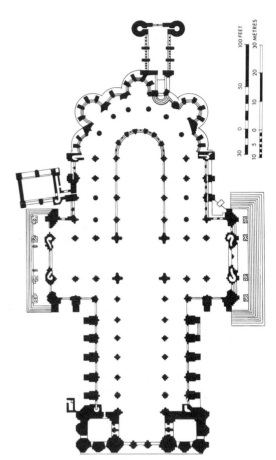

The plan, above, including the alternating radiating chapels, follows the lines of Bishop Fulbert's crypt, sacred to so many pilgrims. The choir and ambulatory, however, were widened and the transepts added, introducing a centralising note.

Right, the interior of Chartres, whose shafted piers, quadripartite vaulting, almost total elimination of wall (and of course flying buttresses) made it the first fully developed Gothic cathedral. The unusual harmony of proportion and the ordered splendour of the windows are unique.

because of the cobalt that was added to the potmetal. The window on the right shows a Tree of Jesse; that on the left the Passion, Crucifixion and Redemption. In the centre are scenes from the childhood and ministry of Christ set in a chequerboard of blue and red medallions, alternately circular and square. The other glass of this period—Notre Dame de la Belle Verrière—is set in a 13th-century window, the second in the south choir aisle. Here, as on the Portail Royal, Mary is depicted as the Queen of Heaven enthroned by the censing angels while she herself enthrones the Infant Christ.

The rest of the glass in the cathedral (except for that belonging to the 14th century in the Chapel of St Piat) is 13th century and represents the largest and finest collection anywhere. The central window of the choir clerestory shows the Virgin, flanked on either side by prophets, New Testament scenes and central episodes from the lives of saints. The figures are full scale, easy to see and mostly donated by the well-to-do. The apsidal chapels feature the lives of the saints to whom they were dedicated and whose relics they probably once contained.

The climax to the glass of Chartres is the three big rose windows. The earliest—that of the west front and devoted to the Last Judgement—begins modestly with small light-toned studs of glass. In the south rose, which represents the same subject, the studs are larger (since they are set in tracery) and the colours richer. Furthermore the lancets below (which are more fully integrated into the design) represent, on either side of the Virgin, the dramatic figures of the four evangelists astride the shoulders of the four major prophets. The north rose, which is the latest of the three and has the most developed tracery, includes a circle of diamonds adding an intoxicated movement to the design. It is dedicated to the Virgin, who appears both in the centre of the rose and as a child seated on the lap of St Anne in the centre lancet, flanked by awe-inspiring figures from the Old Testament.

The sculpture outside shows the same carefully planned scheme apparent in the stained glass; the subject of each portal corresponds to that in the windows above. The designs were drawn up by the clerics and canons of the school attached to the cathedral and were then handed to the sculptors and the craftsmen in stained glass. The school of Chartres was renowned for its broad and cultured Humanism and its interest in Neoplatonic philosophy and in mathematical and musical studies inherited from the time of Fulbert.

84   Chartres abounds in statuary—10,000 figures all of a very high

quality and in an excellent state of preservation. The north transept façade (dating from 1210) is dedicated to the Virgin, and originally consisted only of the centre portal. On the tympanum Mary is shown at the supreme moment of her coronation. Above, in the voussoirs, her lineage is represented by 26 generations of the Tree of Jesse; below are her death and Assumption. On either side are ranged the prophets and other forerunners of Christ from the Old Testament. Finally, at the central doorpost, stands the stately figure of St Anne, the mother of the Virgin—an unusual choice of subject that was probably inspired by the recently acquired relic of her head. The later left portal completes the events of Mary's life, while the right represents characters from the Old Testament, who prefigured the deliverance from ignorance brought about by the Christian Church. Last of all, the porch was added, amplifying the themes of the portals.

The south portal is entirely devoted to the New Testament. In the centre doorway is represented the Last Judgement, slightly earlier than that of Paris. Particularly interesting features are a complete hierarchy of angels in the voussoirs and the beautiful figure of Christ on the central doorpost. Shown in the midst of his apostles as a teacher and preceptor, his expression is sad but shows a humanity unknown to the Beau Dieu of Amiens. The left-hand portal is devoted to the martyrs, and the right to the confessors. Finally, along the breadth of the portals stand close ranks of martyrs, apostles and confessors in silent witness of their faith.

The origin of these column figures dates back to the Abbey of St Denis, where in the 1140s Suger had placed similar figures representing the precursors of Christ (now destroyed) on the splays of the portals. From St Denis the idea spread to Chartres, where the magnificent ensemble of the Portail Royal was carved on the new west façade built at the time of the south tower. Originally this portal stood further back, where the second pair of piers of the present building now stand. Framed and shadowed by the two western towers, the portal must have seemed far more powerful and mysterious than it does in its present position (to which it was removed shortly afterwards). The theme of the Portail Royal is as carefully developed as that of the two later façades, though without the same encyclopedic detail. In the centre is the figure of Christ in Glory, accompanied by the four Beasts of the Apocalypse; above are the 24 elders and below the 12 apostles. This is the Christ of the Second Coming in the Revelation of St John. In the left- and right-hand portals are the other cardinal facts reflecting his Divinity—the

Above, a detail from the centre voussoir of the north porch representing episodes from the Genesis story of the Creation executed with a delightful freshness and economy.

Left, St John the Baptist, one of the jamb figures of the Virgin's porch in the north transept, in which rhythmic curves and play of textures create a figure of melancholy and pathos that has rarely been equalled. 85

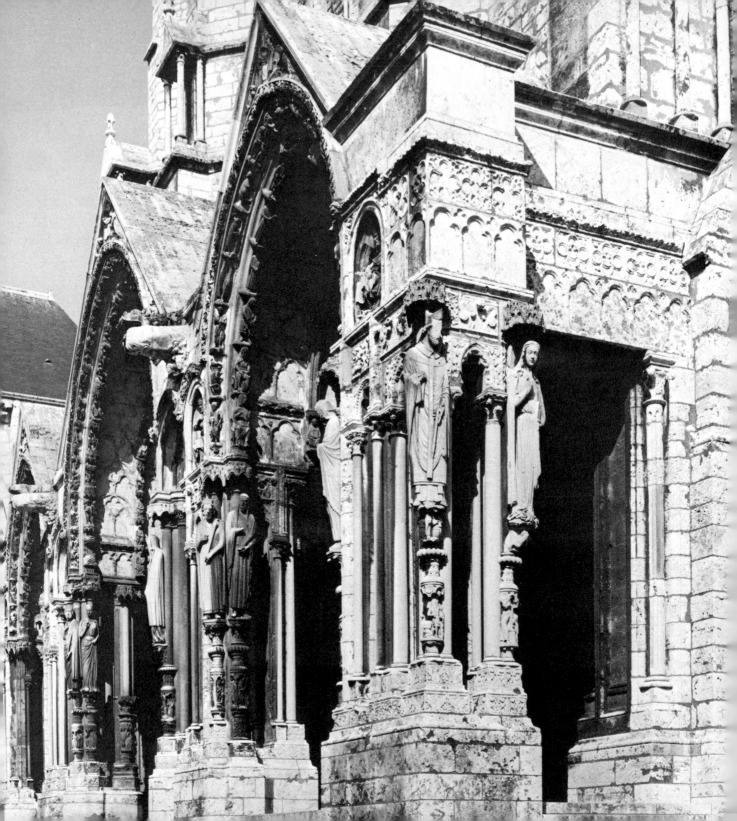

Ascension into heaven and the Nativity or Incarnation. On the capitals are represented all the details of Christ's life on earth, from the story of Joachim and Anna spurned by the High Priest, to his last appearance after his death. The many incidents in this narrative frieze are presented with a piquant urgency; it is as rich in incident as it is richly framed with arcaded canopies and acanthus foliage. In the orders of the arches of the left portal are shown the occupations of the months and the corresponding signs of the Zodiac.

The arches of the right-hand portal are mainly devoted to the liberal arts, or Trivium, and to the mathematical arts, or Quadrivium. These are represented by their great classical exponents—Donatus, Cicero and Aristotle for the first group and Euclid, Boethius, Pythagoras and Ptolemy for the second, and by other corresponding allegorical figures. Thus work, the condition of man's existence and the prerequisite of every Christian, is symbolised on this façade

Opposite, the north porch, whose cavernous arches are resplendent with a myriad of enchanting figures, is also famous for one of the latest statues at Chartres, that of the local martyr St Modeste (extreme right). Her qualities of candour and simple dignity had a far-reaching influence.

The socles below St Modeste and her companion, left, are remarkable for their bizarre forms and for the compressed drama of the scenes that they enclose.

Above, on the right-hand portal of the south transept are the confessors: St Martin (a miracle worker), St Jerome (a Doctor of the Church) and St Gregory (a pope). Note the holy dove whispering into St Gregory's ear while his secretary writes under his feet.

Left, some of the figures representing the witnesses of the new order, ranged along the south transept portals. In the foreground are the martyrs St Vincent, St Denis and St Piat, and St George (added later).

Right, the Portail Royal (c. 1145–55) of the west front, the earliest surviving example of a figured Gothic portal. The zest of its figures, the vigour of its decoration and its closely knit subjects are a wonderful testimony to the religious Renaissance of the 12th century.

Majesty and a new humanity combine in the central tympanum, opposite, from the west front, representing St John's vision of Christ in Glory with the four symbols of the evangelists.

Festive arabesques abound in the tympanum of the Ascension and Pentecost from the Portail Royal, left.

Simple robust figures narrate the bare events of the Virgin's life in the tympanum of the Incarnation, below—a style equally suited to the Liberal Arts of the voussoirs. Note Pythagoras (bottom left) representing music (above him) and Donatus (bottom right) representing grammar (similarly seated above him).

Left, 'the saints before Christ's coming'. Note how their fluted drapery and richly patterned backgrounds blend with the fabric of the church while, as columns, they are part of the structure.

in both its physical and intellectual aspects. Each group is as succinct as an ideograph but still a recognisable portrait of reality. Even more fascinating are the column figures below, whose shrouded and attenuated forms give them the air of disembodied spirits. From what strange world do they emanate? We know that Suger gathered craftsmen from the four corners of France. And when we observe the various adornments, the differing styles of hair and dress and the jungle profusion of patterns behind, abstract, vegetable or alive with beasts and demons, a confluence of a wide variety of cultures becomes evident—Scandinavian, Islamic, Byzantine and classical, all infused and unified by an extraordinary decorative vitality.

Thus, when we consider the cathedral as a whole, a certain lack of unity is apparent in the exterior of the transepts. But this is a minor point when we recall the superb harmony of the jewelled interior and the solemn concourse of redeemed humanity that throngs its portals testifying to a northern rebirth of the great Humanist tradition more 92 than a century before Giotto.

Blazing rubies and mystical blues enriched by the varying quality of the glass and light lend a living quality to the hieratic Queen of Heaven, right, from the famous window known as Notre Dame de la Belle Verrière.

CHAPTER 6

REIMS

Today the cathedral of Reims is approached by a wide avenue of lime trees terminating in a circular open space—a much grander setting than that planned by its medieval builders. Nevertheless, the cathedral is so majestic that its formal approach enhances it without isolating it into a monument. Reims is a major city, and any other surroundings to the coronation church of France would be incongruous.

This grandeur is apparent in every stone of the fabric, from the rich profusion of its summer foliage crowning both the inside and outside capitals to the festive throngs of angels, some flying up the buttresses of the apse chapels, others garlanding the church with their outstretched wings; others still, archangels, have descended to ground level and appear on the jambs of the portals. On every niche, gallery or ledge perches a saint, prophet or king—figures that even inhabit the gables and crown the spire. The building pulsates with life, bursting into bud up the pinnacles or into hedges of parapeting along the eaves of the roofs. The elegant moulded forms of the flying buttresses are as far removed from the square-cut hunks of Chartres as the structure of the windows, whose tracery consists of the same sinews as the system of ribs inside, is from the juxtaposed units punched out of an inert wall at Chartres. Almost every unit is moulded in relief, so that exterior and interior mingle together.

The cathedral of Reims is, however, more than an enriched specimen of the High Gothic style. It has classical qualities that make it unique among Gothic buildings. Although two hundred years were needed to complete its façade, complete symmetry was maintained. The decorative details are also unusually uniform. The same pattern of geometrical tracery is used in all the windows, the same pinnacled

tabernacles, the same foliage, mostly a five-fingered type on the capitals and in the rectangles that decorate the inside of the west wall. A sense of stability is another characteristic. This is produced not so much by the sheer mass of masonry as by the width added to the ground storey of the façade by two blind portals, which were copied from the rival church of St Nicaise at Reims. In the same way, the interior is characterised by a powerful upward thrust, but without the impression of strain created at Amiens, Beauvais and Cologne. To these classical virtues should be added the bold design of the façade, which makes Amiens look cluttered and the transepts of Chartres only just co-ordinated. However, the classical character of Reims is most apparent in the portal sculpture. This impression is created not

Far left, the west front of Reims Cathedral, which combines a classical stability and symmetry with a sense of organic growth, and a largeness of design with pulsating detail; its regal magnificence admirably suits its role of France's coronation cathedral.

The east end of the cathedral, left, is made up of a basis of geometric shapes overlaid by a wealth of moulded and figured forms. The battlemented parapet of the apse and some of the animals below are replacements designed by Viollet-le-Duc.

only by the obvious influence of antique models both in the individual figures and in the motif below (unique to Reims) of the classical drapes but also by the relationship of the component parts—canopies, foliage, figures, columns and drapes—to one another. The seething jungle of life on the columns of the Portail Royal at Chartres has been replaced by a sense of space and interval. The canopies no longer represent whole towns in miniature, but consist of a regular succession of arcades as abstract as the rhythm of the drapes below. As a result, the intervening figures and frieze of foliage have assumed a new value.

The spirit of uniformity that invests the cathedral of Reims is partly due to the total rebuilding after the fire of 1200. The earliest church at Reims was built around 400 by Bishop Nicasius, who was later martyred by the Vandals before its porch. In this church St Remi anointed Clovis king of the Franks with holy oil, which, it is said, came down with the dew from heaven. Ever since Reims has been the coronation church of the kings of France. The present building was begun only a year after the fire, and work continued without a pause for twenty years. By 1241 the choir and transepts were complete and the chapter moved in. The nave was then started, but by 1257 so many debts had accumulated that the pope issued a bull urging the secular and monastic clergy of the archdiocese to contribute funds to their cathedral. By 1285 the nave must have been completed and the west front built up as high as the storey of the big rose. Jean d'Orbais, Jean le Loup, Gaucher de Reims and Bernard de Soissons were the master-masons responsible. This is the first instance among French cathedrals where such information has come down to us.

During the Hundred Years War work on the cathedral slowed down, though it never completely stopped. By about 1400, the cathedral was complete except for the upper stages of the towers. Charles VI then gave permission for stone to be collected for these from any land within a radius of four leagues, even from cultivated fields or vineyards. Finally, in 1427, the two towers were completed. Two years later, on July 17, 1429, one of the most momentous episodes in the cathedral's history took place. Charles VII, previously merely the *roi de Bourges*, was anointed king of France while Joan of Arc knelt behind him in shimmering armour holding the standard that she had borne across France from Orléans at the head of his victorious army.

Maintenance work on the cathedral began long before the work of

One of the arches of the inside wall of the west front showing part of the magnificent trellis of figures and foliage. Originally this was probably gilded to set off the stained glass of the rose.

The garland of angels and rich tufting of the parapet lend a festive air to the view, left, of the south side of the nave. Note the bar tracery of the windows, an innovation of Reims.

Below, a 17th-century engraving of St Nicaise of Reims (begun in 1231 and destroyed in 1798), showing the probable origin of the multiple gabled base of the cathedral and the motif of the rose enclosed in the pointed arch—a reconciliation of favourite but conflicting Gothic designs.

Viollet-le-Duc in the 19th century. In the 17th and 18th centuries the cathedral (unlike others) still earned respect and admiration for its symmetry and figures were being replaced on the arches of its main portals. The chalky limestone (whose topsoil nourishes the champagne grape) of which Reims is built is more resistant to weathering than might be imagined. The battered appearance of the cathedral is largely the result of the fire of 1914 and the damage inflicted during the 1914–18 War.

What innovations were made at Reims? The form of the flying buttresses and the bar tracery of the windows have already been mentioned as significant developments since Chartres. The piers too have evolved. Those at Chartres, though logical, had a confused appearance produced by the varied projections of the abacus. At Reims, the abacus of the central core is still set diagonally, but the projections that receive the orders of the arcade and the vaulting shafts of the transverse ribs of the nave and aisles are now all 98 polygonal. The capitals too are simplified, being united into one zone; any change in size is masked by the luxuriant band of foliage. The piers also do not alternate in design. Reims was begun 15 years after Chartres, and was based on the same plan, except that three more bays were added to the nave and the transepts and choir reduced by one bay. Unlike Chartres, the chapels round the choir do not alternate and only the chapel on the axis is more pronounced. The internal elevation is based on the scheme of Chartres, but the arcade and vaults are higher and all the ribs are pointed. There is therefore less pressure on the buttresses, which are more slender in their forms.

The mouldings at Reims are still simple. They consist of a plain roll on a flat projection, and needed little light to show them to advantage. The windows of the choir and transepts, like all stained glass before 1260, were intense and dark in tone. Today little remains; the glass in the aisles and chapels was removed in the 18th century and the rest was badly damaged during the 1914–18 War. Most of the glass in the clerestory, however, is medieval: that at the head of the choir depicts Christ on the Cross with Mary and John; below is a contemporary portrait of Archbishop Henri de Braine (1227–40) and, to the left, the Virgin and Child above the Metropolitan Church. On either side are apostles and evangelists and suffragan bishops holding models of their cathedrals. The 13th-century north rose represents the Creation of the World, the south rose made in 1581 (a year after a storm had blown out its predecessor) Jesus surrounded by apostles. The windows in the nave clerestory date from the second half of the 13th century, but now only show the eight kings of France and the bishops who consecrated them. Finally, in the west rose, is the Virgin surrounded by angels, kings and patriarchs and below, in the triforium lancets, the Coronation of Clovis. The rose beneath is a modern work by Jacques Simon, who also designed the Window of the Winegrowers in the transept. Here in the clerestory are some unusual grisaille windows dating from the 13th century.

The sculpture at Reims is superbly integrated with the architecture, whose simple classical forms provide the perfect setting for its luxuriant vegetation and noble figures. On the inside of the west wall is a trellis design that combines the two. Seven rows of niches set in rectangles of foliage and enclosing individual figures rise to the height of the door, which is as high as the nave arcade. Those on the right relate the story of St John the Baptist, who prophesied the coming of a Messiah, and those on the right portray this coming. The narrative

The plan of Reims is based on that of Chartres, though the eastern parts are more centralised and the nave is longer—probably to accommodate the congregation and procession during the coronation ceremony.

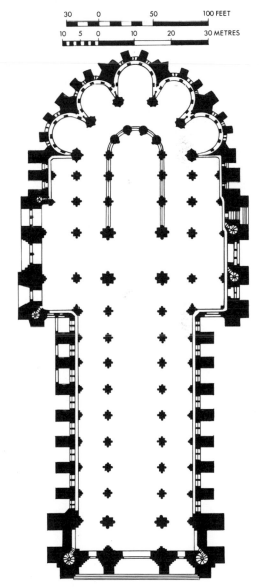

30   0   50   100 FEET

10 5 0   10   20   30 METRES

99

pe\`ci une \`def fo\`mef \`de\`rainf
\`cef e\`fpa\`cef \`de la nef telef co\`m
\`def funt en\`tre tʒ pi\`lerf.
\`iestoie mandef en le te\`rre \`de
\`hongrie qant io le po\`rtraif
po\`co\`r la\`mai io mi\`ex.

*Above, one of the capitals of the nave depicting
a genre scene of grape picking among a tangle of
fig and vine leaves.*

*Left, one of the aisle windows at Reims drawn by
Villard de Honnecourt 'because I liked it best'—
one of a dozen drawings he made of the cathedral while it was being built.*

*Opposite, the arcades and vaults of the nave at
Reims (begun 1211), which though the loftiest
of their time, soar without strain. The great
rose windows, moulded tracery and generous use
of foliage complete the impression of effortless
and gracious harmony.* 101

Above, a frieze of resurrecting figures (c. 1225–40) from the tympanum of the north transept, which owes its liveliness to the pattern of varied silhouettes and empty spaces. Note the urns, one of the many indications at the cathedral of the presence of antique remains in the neighbourhood.

A close observation of nature and strong architectonic qualities unite in the trellis of foliage and figure niches (c. 1270), left, which lines the inside wall of the west front.

runs from the bottom upwards and each episode is condensed into a
single figure, which adds an epic quality to the intimate realism of the
fields of leaves. These include at least thirty different kinds of plant
and flower—ivy, vine, wild briar, hawthorn, thistle and mallow, to
name a few. Curiously this trellis and figure design has no obvious
predecessor, or indeed a successor of any significance. The design
continues round the aisle doors, linking the subjects of the portals
outside. Unfortunately, it is badly mutilated.

The earliest of the outside sculpture is the enthroned Virgin on
the tympanum of the right-hand door of the north transept. As
delicate as a carving in ivory, it is close in style to the Virgin of the
Portail St Anne at Paris. The little 'soul' cradled by two angels in
the arch above suggests that it was originally part of a tomb dating

103

from the end of the 12th century, which was probably rescued from the earlier Carolingian church. The doorway to the left is devoted to the Last Judgement. On its splays are six apostles, stocky types showing obvious classical influence; in the centre is the figure of Christ, similar to the Beau Dieu of Amiens, though less austere. The tympanum is remarkable for the two rows of resurrected figures, each a lithe young body in the prime of life. The centre portal is entirely dedicated to local saints. The centre figure is usually identified with St Sixtus, who introduced Christianity to France and was the first bishop of Reims. On the left jamb is St Nicaisius burdened with his decapitated head but rewarded with the crown of martyrdom. To the right is the companion of his martyrdom, his siter Eutropia, and to the left a censing angel. The right jamb shows St Remi receiving the holy phial of oil accompanied by Job and flanked by an angel on either side. On the tympanum are episodes from the lives of the two saints in a later style, dating from the middle of the century. In the niches above the buttresses are statues of kings of France and close to the rose window on either side are the clothed figures of Adam and Eve, who caresses a delightful dragon. The south transept is doorless, but on either side of the rose are figures symbolising the Church and Synagogue, which foreshadow those of Strasbourg.

Passing to the west front, at the top crossing the central gable and encircling the towers is a row of kings, possibly of France and not of Judah, since they include a representation of Clovis's baptism. Lower down, above the rose, are giant statues of David and Goliath and the two pilgrims of Emmaus. The niches of the first storey of the towers house saints, martyrs and a beautiful representation of Christ and Doubting Thomas.

The sculpture of Reims covers a wide range in style from the archaic figures of the right portal to the antique-type statues of the north transept, the Visitation and the figure of Isaiah. The group comprising the Virgin of the Annunciation and Presentation, the old man Simeon, St Nicaisius and several other figures on the left door of the west front and various angels and kings higher on the building are inspired by the sculpture at Amiens. But the most beautiful figures belong to the fourth and latest group, which is the creation of Reims and includes the figures inside the west wall, the pilgrims of Emmaus, Christ and Doubting Thomas, the Eve of the north transept and some of the angels and kings. This collection also includes the debonair St Joseph, the wordly Anna, the smiling angel who announces the news to Mary and the other more mysterious

104

Above, the tragic headless figure of St Nicasius, accompanied by a censing angel and the companion of his martyrdom, his sister Eutropia, from the centre portal of the north transept. The influence of classical antiquity and the bands of foliage are already found in these early figures (c. 1125–40).

Serene and poised, the famous groups of the Annunciation and Visitation, right, exchange their solemn greetings. Note the three different styles, all of an equally high quality: the first derives from antique statuary (the Visitation group), another from Amiens (the Annunciate Virgin), while the angel is peculiar to Reims.

angel who ministers to St Nicaisius. Positioning marks by masons show that some statues were rearranged. The early figures of the precursors, for instance, were moved from their more usual position on the Virgin's portal to that of the Last Judgement.

In the figures of Reims we meet for the first time a race of beings stirred by a new life that pervades their whole bodies; the figures of Chartres by comparison look almost repressed. And they comprise, like the leaves that surround them, a variety of types. Isolated examples of this new awareness are found in earlier cathedrals, but at Reims it permeates the whole building. Its influence was widespread; the foliage reappears at Naumburg and in the chapter house at Southwell, the figures in the Vierge Dorée of Amiens and in the statues of Bamberg and Strasbourg; and the architecture in another coronation church, Westminster Abbey. A vital factor in this influence must have been the unity of style at Reims, where for the first time the Gothic had developed to a stage where the exterior is expressed in the same language of forms as the interior.

Above, a close-up of the angel affectionately known as Le Sourire de Reims—*the first smiling figure in stone to introduce a note of mystery.*

The sense of interval apparent throughout Reims gives extra value to the striking characterisations of Joseph and Anna in the Presentation group, opposite, on the centre portal of the west front. 107

Purpose, precision and economy are the guiding principles of the skeletal structure of Amiens. Yet the fillet mouldings and traceried arcading to the buttresses (left) are purely decorative.

Inside the same chasteness prevails. Clean-cut mouldings are accentuated by the flood of light, interrupted by a minimum of decoration. Every line soars to the unprecedented height of 140 feet, surpassed only by Beauvais; the relation of width to height is 1:3, again exceeded only by Beauvais, which is 1:3.4 and by Cologne, which is 1:3.8. One item in particular checks this vertical drive, directing our eyes equally urgently towards the altar. This is the garland of deeply undercut foliage that runs along the base of the triforium around the nave, transepts and choir. It also pulls the soaring lines together, acting as a visible counterpart to the hidden chain of tie-rods that was inserted into the passage of the triforium as a safety measure during the 14th century. Above the garland, the vertical lines continue upwards; triforium and clerestory become joined by the central mullion of the window. In the choir built during a second campaign, the triforium is glazed, thus reducing the area above the main arcade to virtually one unit. Again the detail is significant: all the finishing or starting units are polygonal, the bases and abaci of the piers are octagonal; and those of the triforium colonettes hexagonal. The bases of the diagonal and wall ribs are also hexagonal, all as precise and neat as the footwork of a ballet dancer.

The west front of Amiens is disappointing. The clean lines and refinement of detail found in the rest of the building are absent here. The general disposition recalls the façade of Notre Dame in

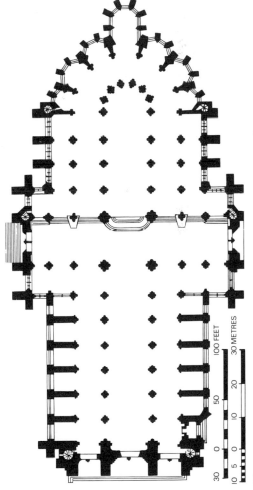

Opposite, a 19th-century engraving, which clearly conveys the dizzy height (140 feet) of Amiens. The almost total removal of the stained glass enhances the austere character of the cathedral.

In spite of its lack of decorative unity, the façade of Amiens, left, has a certain prim stateliness.

Below, a plan of Amiens, even more centralised than that of Reims.

113

Paris, but the two superimposed galleries, which run across the centre of the front, detract from the impact made by the rose window. The towers too (especially from the side) are inadequate tokens of strength. On the other hand, the cavernous depths of the portals are impressive, the double rows of quatrefoils on the plinths delightful and the flamboyant tracery of the rose exquisite. But there is a lack of unity in the decoration of the whole. This is partly because of the enthusiastic additions by Viollet-le-Duc. Another reason may be that Amiens was built from west to east, so that perhaps the façade was roughed out too quickly or maybe even took shape before the essence of the nave design had been fully appreciated.

The present building follows the same pattern as that of its contemporaries. It was built to replace a 12th-century church gutted by fire in 1218, which was itself the third church to occupy the site. No part of these earlier buildings remains. The foundation stone was laid in 1220 by Bishop Evrard de Fouilloy, whose bronze tomb lies in the floor of the nave. The plan is the work of Robert de Luzarches, the first master-mason, who was succeeded (probably in 1258) by Thomas de Cormont and later by his son Renaud.

Construction started at the west end, so that the church of St Firmin to the east could still be used for services. By 1236 the nave was complete and the west front erected up to the frieze above the rose window; the statues of the portals were also in place and the transepts had been started. In 1238 the choir was begun and by 1247 the ambulatory and apsidal chapels were finished. In 1258 the upper parts of the choir and transepts were started (probably under Thomas de Cormont) and in the same year a fire broke out, damaging all the unfinished parts of the cathedral. By 1269 these were finished, the stained glass inserted into the apse and the relics of St Firmin translated with great ceremony in the presence of the young Prince Edward of England. In 1290 the first of the side chapels was built into the angle of the south transept and the nave, followed by another chapel in the corresponding area on the north side. The remaining spaces between the buttresses of the nave were successively converted into chapels throughout the 14th century, a practice that fortunately was not followed at Chartres and Reims. Less than a century later Amiens Cathedral, universally regarded as the summit of Gothic achievement, was already undergoing repairs. Apart from earlier reinforcements to the north tower, the fabric had to be strengthened by several piers in the north aisle of the choir and by the rebuilding of these aisle vaults. Then, to redress the outward thrust made by the piers of the central crossing, the chain of tie-rods already mentioned was inserted.

So much for the visual appearance and history of Amiens. What were the innovations made by Robert de Luzarches? Though the language of its forms is different from that of Jean d'Orbais of Reims, the plan of Amiens was modelled on that cathedral, which had been begun 11 years earlier and was still being built. Both cathedrals are about the same length, only at Amiens the crossing is more-or-less at the centre, though, perhaps to reassert the west–east axis, the central apsidal chapel has been prolonged. The most obvious difference between the two cathedrals is the reduced thickness of the walls at Amiens. Other important technical differences are found in the disposition of the component parts of the piers and in the tracery. Compared with the piers of Chartres, those at Amiens are handled more elegantly, the principal shaft rising from floor to vault broken only by a ring. The shafts of the piers of the central crossing, where

there is no arcade, rise without interruption to their full height, expressing a unity that after Amiens appears in the main shafts of all piers in future cathedrals. The fusion of triforium and clerestory into one unit of design is also new, as is the elaboration of the tracery. Because less stone was used, more supports were necessary. At Amiens, three mullions replace the single one at Reims, and an eight-foiled window the earlier sexfoiled. Another development, which was to have far-reaching influence, is the refinement of the mouldings. In the arches of the arcade and aisles a fillet has been added to the roll, sharpening the line of the whole moulding, which is pear-shape in section. In the triforium the fillet has been given a keel section, resulting in a double curve both concave and convex, an instance of the ogee curve that was such a characteristic feature of the late Gothic style.

These details were shown to full advantage by the flood of light let in through the vast glazed areas. Little remains today of the original stained glass, but all that in the east of the church was probably light in tonality, since this was the trend of the time.

Luckily the sculpture has suffered comparatively little, for the west front contains an encyclopedic review of 13th-century belief, knowledge and activity. Executed in an unusually consistent style between 1220–5 and 1236, it is a little later than that at Chartres (with which it has occasional similarities) and Paris. Central to the whole scheme is the Last Judgement, which is unfolded on the principal portal and is similar to those of the other great cathedrals. And unique to this cathedral is the parable of the Fruitful Tree and the Axed Tree, which appears on the door frame below the Wise and Foolish Virgins as further symbols of vigilance. Ranged along the jambs are the twelve apostles and four major prophets, whose untroubled gaze is fixed on distant horizons. In their midst on the central pier is Christ, Le Beau Dieu, his right arm raised in blessing and his left holding the Bible. Under his feet are the lion and the dragon mentioned in Psalm XC; below to the left and the right are the basilisk and the adder, also referred to by the psalmist. According to the contemporary writer Honorius of Autun, the basilisk represents death and the adder 'the sinner who closes his ears to the words of life'. The sides of the pier are decorated with a pattern of abstract daisies, neat and chaste. This motif covers the plinth of the entire west front and is in perfect harmony with the spirit of Amiens.

116   The final item in this scheme, in a format reminiscent of Moorish

With one hand holding the Bible and the other raised in blessing, the Beau Dieu of Amiens is both the teaching and the triumphant Christ. The purity and simplicity of his countenance and the surrounding pattern of daisies are equally characteristic of the spirit of Amiens.

Right, quatrefoils on the central buttresses depicting the prophecies of Zephaniah and Habakkuk placed below their appropriate prophets.

Left, two quatrefoils representing the prophecy: '. . . and they shall beat their swords into plowshares, and their spears into pruninghooks: nation shall not lift up a sword against nation, neither shall they learn war any more.' (Micah iv. 1.)

Right, three signs of the Zodiac—Capricorn, Aquarius and Pisces—with the labours of the month below: December preparing a carcase for a winter feast; January feasting; and February seated by a fire with his boots off.

tiles, is the double row of quatrefoils running round the buttresses and into the porches. In the centre (as was usual in representations of the Last Judgement), they show the 12 virtues and vices selected and illustrated as at Paris, but here beginning with a fable from Aesop. On the buttresses below the prophets, the quatrefoils relate their visions in scenes full of a picturesque charm far removed from the Hebraic imagery of the Bible. On the Virgin's porch on the right they again illustrate episodes from the lives of figures above them: prefigurations from the Old Testament of the Virgin Birth, similar to those at Laon, scenes from the childhood of St John the Baptist and of Christ, events in the story of the Magi (including their journey home in a boat set alight by the agents of Herod) and finally the story of King Solomon and the Queen of Sheba. On the portal of St Firmin on the left, the quatrefoils show the signs of the Zodiac and a corresponding scene for each of the months below, perhaps the most delightful series found in any cathedral.

The Virgin's porch shows her death, Assumption and Coronation on the tympanum, which, like the Last Judgement, shows a close familiarity with the same scene at Paris and Chartres. The Annunciation, Visitation and the Presentation are enacted by the standing figures of the right-hand splay, some of the most beautiful at Amiens. The simple planes of the drapery and the homely features express the unaffected good-humour that is peculiar to the cathedral.

A generation later, around 1255–60, a tympanum carved in a very different style was added to the façade of the south transept. The figures are lively, the line crisp, and there is new feeling for the value of space. On the lintel, the apostles stand in pairs in animated conversation; in the four registers above is represented the life of St Honorius. And on the central pier stands the famous Vierge Dorée, described by Ruskin as the soubrette of Amiens. Here the Queen of Heaven has been brilliantly portrayed as a coquettish figure of fashion (whose beauty was once gilded and glistening) with a trio of small angels to adjust the tilt of her elegant halo.

The prevailing spirit of Amiens is that of Robert de Luzarches and the original builders who created the Beau Dieu, the flying buttresses and the soaring vaults. At Amiens, the Gothic style of the Ile de France was finally perfected and set the pattern for countless cathedrals all over Europe from Beauvais, Troyes and Tours in the north of France and Clermont-Ferrand, Limoges, Narbonne, Rodez and Toulouse in the south to Cologne, Antwerp, and as far afield as Prague and Uppsala.

Unlike Reims, the Annunciation, Visitation and Presentation are here represented by figures that seem to belong to the same sober and good-humoured family, identically clothed in simply draped garments.

121

CHAPTER 8

CANTERBURY

Neither jostled by the surrounding town nor entirely secluded from it, the site of Canterbury Cathedral achieves a happy compromise. Partly concealed by the tiled roofs, painted gables and brick-fronted houses in mellow reds that nestle beneath it, the cathedral is best seen by approaching either from the north-east, through the flint gate known as the Dark Entry, or from the south-west, through Christchurch Gate into the precincts. Even from there the vast scale of this towering structure in Caen stone is revealed only from the west end up to the western transepts.

In general design and period the cathedral first evokes Beverley Minster and York Cathedral, yet compared to them its forms are sturdy and scantily decorated. The only patterns are the rectilinear forms of the Perpendicular tracery and the pinnacles of the skyline composed of a few tiers of gablets arranged in cone formation and devoid of any foliage. Further exploration of the close gradually reveals an eastern arm almost twice the length of the nave. Indeed its total length of 547 feet surpassed all other cathedrals at the time it was built (with the possible exception of old St Paul's). This eastern arm starts at the western transept and across it are strung a more deeply projecting eastern transept, then a pair of chapels (both in the Norman style); it finally terminates in the Trinity Chapel and Corona built in the transitional style of the early Gothic. The general effect of the whole is one of bold and simple staccato forms, which have been maintained throughout the history and restoration of the building. On the north side, interlocking with the projecting forms of the cathedral, is a complex of monastic buildings, of which a large number have survived and are now occupied by King's
School.

Like the exterior, the interior of the cathedral has no vantage point from which it can be appreciated as a whole. More than in any other cathedral, the choir, nave and crypt remain three distinct architectural experiences, linked only by flights of stairs. The largest unit, comprising the early Gothic choir, the Trinity Chapel and Corona, has the noble simplicity and stability of a classical building with an added quality of lightness and lucidity. Slim, antique-type columns (the coupled ones 17 times thinner than those of Durham!) support walls enlivened by shafts that rise to meet the dome-like forms of the embracing vault. The sexpartite compartments suggest an umbrella in the last stage of being opened.

A narrow doorway in the pulpitum at the top of a broad flight of

The metropolitan cathedral of Canterbury, whose extraordinary length, offset by bold towers, staccato buttresses and, at the east end, the cliff-like Chapel of Corona add up to a powerful and imposing composition. Note the beautiful Bell Harry Tower, successor to the angel steeple, a famous landmark for pilgrims.

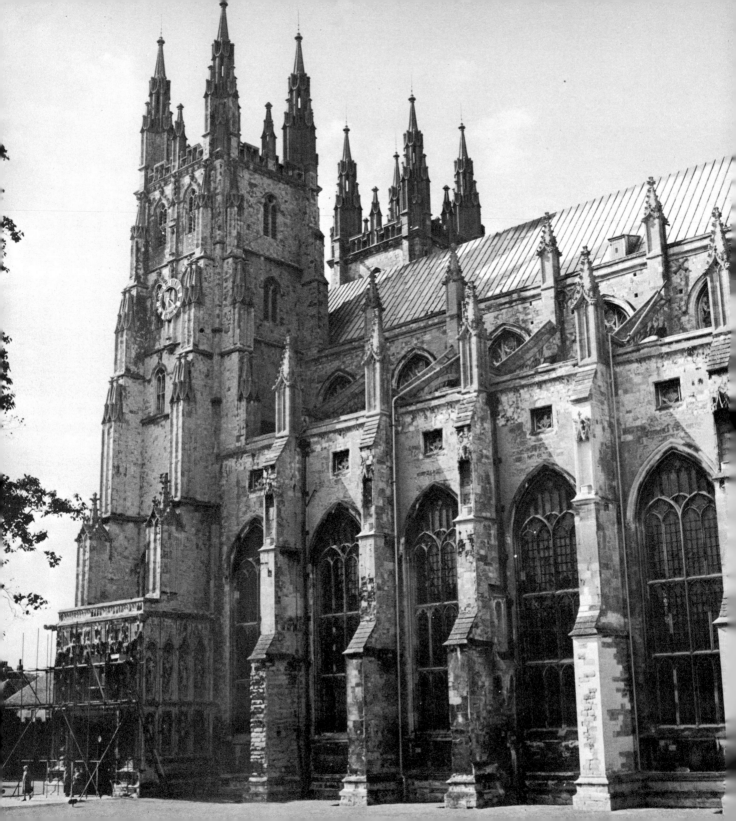

steps provides one of the most breathtaking views of medieval architecture—here is the nave, spacious and unified as a hall, yet reminiscent of an avenue of trees with slender piers that shoot up unchecked and spread their branches over our heads to form crisp star patterns. A further flight of steps brings us to the crypt, the largest example dating from the Romanesque period.

In the crypt the feeling is of seclusion and intimate drama. The groined vaulting is only a few feet above our heads, yet the vistas continue out of sight. And on the capitals is a whole underworld of exultant demons and monsters, the pioneer essays of Anglo-Norman masons into figurative sculpture. (Yet earlier the Saxons had shown considerable skill in representing the human figure, as is shown in the fragment from the ninth-century Reculver cross shaft, which lies in a case near by.) The inspiration for this pagan imagery came largely from the flourishing school of manuscript illumination at Canterbury. But the monsters and demons in the manuscripts do not stray beyond the initials or foliage borders that surround the central religious theme; here they are placed at eye level in the sanctity of the crypt. The school of sculpture initiated at Canterbury in the second decade of the 12th century spread over a wide area of southern England. Compared with French sculpture at this time, there is a curious lack of Christian inspiration.

In the bowels of the crypt there are probably vestiges of the cathedral founded by St Augustine when he was sent by Pope Gregory to England in 547 on a mission of conversion; this cathedral was staffed with secular canons. At the same time, St Augustine founded an abbey close by, which though now in ruins provides a fascinating survey of the growth of early medieval architecture in England; it also shows the most complete monastic layout of the time that has been excavated this side of the Alps.

After a fire in 1067 the cathedral was rebuilt under the 70-year-old Lombard Abbot Lanfranc; at the same time, the cathedral was converted into a Benedictine foundation. This cathedral took only seven years to build, but was only half the size of the present building; its three-apsed choir terminated after the present western transepts. Fragments can be seen in the north-west transept and a few columns survive in the crypt. In 1096, under St Anselm, Prior Ernulf followed by Prior Conrad rebuilt the choir, extending it further east and adding a second eastern transept and an ambulatory stretching round the choir, from which the two chapels of St Andrew and St Anselm (both of which survive today) were set at a tangent.

Above, the nave (1379–1405) by Henry Yevele, which, with its lofty arcade, slender shafts and crisp star patterns of the vaults, is one of the most elegant and spacious interiors created during the middle ages.

Left, the nave and towers, built in the Perpendicular style of the turn of the 14th and 15th centuries. Even so, the influence of the bold rectilinear forms of the Anglo-Norman and Early English eastern parts prevailed throughout the four centuries of Canterbury's history. 125

The fire of 1174 and the increasing number of pilgrims led to the building of the spacious and noble choir, opposite, in the most up-to-date Gothic style, imported by the mason William of Sens from the metropolitan cathedral of his home town.

Left, the crypt (begun in 1096 as a stronghold for relics) whose gloom, seclusion and pagan capitals recall how long the 'darkness' of the middle ages persisted.

Also surviving are the towers that rise at the angles of the eastern transepts, the arcading of the choir aisles and the western crypt. Thomas à Becket celebrated his first mass in the Chapel of the Holy Trinity of this choir and was murdered in 1170 in the north-west transept (now known as the Martydom). He was canonised in 1173, and in 1174 Henry II came to do penance for the rash burst of temper that led to his death, walking barefoot to the cathedral, undergoing the scourge and passing an all-night vigil at his tomb. Thus was launched the most popular pilgrimage in England. Among the many pilgrims was Louis VII, the only French king ever to set foot in England. Henry IV had himself buried next to the shrine of St Thomas—the only royal tomb of Canterbury. He also built a chantry chapel for himself, dedicated to Edward the Confessor. At this time,

Above, an example (from St Gabriel's Chapel) of the unabashed paganism of the crypt capitals. The beading, interweaving and general verve were inspired by Canterbury's illuminated manuscripts.

127

Europe was undergoing a period of piety following the Black Death and the pilgrimages to Canterbury reached their peak. The city council calculated that during the Jubilee Year of 1420 they received 100,000 visitors. A decade or two earlier the group of 29 pilgrims immortalised by Chaucer made their way from London. All these pilgrims provided the cathedral with a handsome income.

Two months after Henry II had done penance a fire destroyed the choir of Conrad. The desolation of the monks and the deliberations that followed were chronicled by one of them named Gervase in one of the most interesting documents to have survived from this period. He writes of the summoning of artificers both French and English and how finally one called William of Sens was retained. After surveying the burnt fabric for many days, he decided at last to confess to the monks that the choir would have to be totally destroyed. Five years later, Gervase tells how during the 'turning of the great vault' William fell 50 feet from the scaffolding. Reclining in bed, the master continued to supervise the work until his return to France, when his place was taken by William the Englishman, 'small in body' writes Gervase, 'but in workmanship of many kinds acute and honest'. William rebuilt the Trinity Chapel and the Corona and at the same time extended the crypt. The next works in the cathedral were smaller. First, screens were erected to separate the choir from the traffic of pilgrims in the aisles and the lower half of the chapter house was built, both between 1304–20. Then, under the south-east transept, the chantry chapel of the Black Prince (now the Huguenot Church) was begun in 1363, which was followed between 1372–7 by the Lady Chapel of the crypt.

Between 1379 and 1405 Lanfranc's Early Norman nave and the south transept were rebuilt (it must have looked as primitive as that of St Alban's). The principal master associated with the rebuilding was Henry Yevele, who appears to have been the most distinguished architect of the 14th century as well as being a man of considerable property.

Finally new towers were erected, that of the south-west between 1423–34 by Thomas Mapilton (designer of Durham cloisters). Its twin on the north-west belongs to the mid-19th century, together with the figures decorating the 15th-century 'welcoming porch' at the south-west corner. Then between 1493–7 the crowning feature of Canterbury was built—Bell Harry Tower over the central crossing, designed by John Wastell, a Canterbury man and the architect of

King's College Chapel, Cambridge. It replaced an earlier steeple

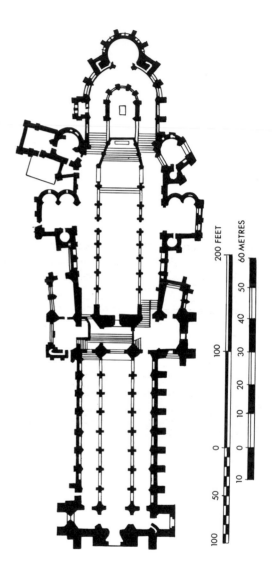

The plan of Canterbury, above, is principally notable for its then unprecedented length of 547 feet; the eastern parts are nearly twice the length of the nave. Note too the double transepts.

topped by a gilded angel, a landmark for pilgrims on their way to the shrine. Built on to the base of Lanfranc's tower, its core is made of brick—a light material that was easy to manufacture and erect. The tower is 235 feet high and is surpassed only by Lincoln, which is 271.

The most novel of the many items at Canterbury was the choir. It was a direct copy of the most up-to-date French Gothic of the time, mostly from Sens, though the marble shafting derives from Valenciennes. Even so, distinct English modifications are noticeable. Because of the old choir's historical associations and the survival of the two apsidal chapels and the eastern transepts, the old foundations were kept. Hence its rambling length. The Anglo-Norman fondness for thick walls is apparent in the double layers of the clerestory; further buttressing of the vaults was performed by the transverse arches concealed under the triforium roof and the curious rudimentary flyers above it. The other English feature is the profusion of Purbeck marble. In the choir it is confined to the vaulting shafts

Below left, the Byzantine figure of St Paul shaking off the viper (c. 1150), a magnificent example of the extensive frescoes that once covered Conrad's Norman church.

Below, the tomb of the Black Prince, who lies surrounded by a crenellated enclosure in the characteristically rigid pose of effigies after the Black Death.

129

and the colonettes of the gallery, while beyond the eastern transepts it is added to the compound piers. In the Trinity Chapel, all the coupled columns are made of Purbeck especially selected for their rich and varied colouring.

An influential aspect of Canterbury is the double transept plan adopted by Ernulf and Conrad. Based on the recently enlarged mother church of the Benedictine order at Cluny, it must have made a tremendous impact, and though almost unknown on the continent, it reappears in England at the beginning of the 13th century, first at Lincoln and then at Hereford, Salisbury, Worcester, Southwell and Durham.

Today Canterbury's most unusual possession is its early stained glass. Its similarity to the glass at St Denis, Chartres and Sens suggests that it was made by the same atelier of glaziers working over a period of 70 years. The earliest glass is in the choir clerestory, which was filled (while the scaffolding was still up) with a genealogical series beginning in the north-west with the Creation of Adam and ending with Mary and Christ. Only nine of these bold figures still remain; the rest have been replaced with modern replicas. In the centre of the apse there is a break in the sequence to allow for three windows depicting the Life and Passion of Christ. Also 12th-century are the two delicate and unusual rose windows of the eastern transepts. The north rose represents the Old Dispensation of the Law and the Prophets executed in white and a range of blues and pinks, picked up lower down in the colours of the triforium windows. The south rose illustrates the New Dispensation of Christ and the Church, in which the shades of tan replace the pinks; the figures are the work of the Victorian restorer George Austin Junior. Below are new windows by Erwin Bossanyi, whose stimulating colours are slightly overpowering so close to the sharp youthful forms of the early Gothic arcading.

The two theological windows of the north choir aisle belong to the turn of the 12th and 13th centuries—all that remain of a dozen windows that once extended into the eastern transepts. They are similar in arrangement (and as esoteric in subject-matter) to the windows of the New Alliance of Chartres and Bourges. The centre medallions illustrate the principal theme and those on the side represent glosses from the Old Testament. Several parables are depicted—a rare choice of subject (except for the Good Samaritan and the Prodigal Son) in the middle ages. Fragments exist from the Parable of the Sower (Window I, panels 15 and 20) showing the seed

The cloisters, founded in 1073 and reconstructed in 1236, were remodelled in 1397–1414 when the rich lierne vaulting with heraldic shields was added.

131

Left, the Trinity Chapel, where, surrounded by Purbeck columns with acanthus foliage on a glossy pavement of opus alexandrinum, *stood the fabulous shrine of St Thomas à Becket, the goal of every pilgrim to Canterbury.*

Opposite, the interior of the metropolitan cathedral of Sens, begun in 1140, and among the earliest in the Gothic style. Here can be seen the prototype of Canterbury's coupled columns with acanthus capitals, small gallery and sexpartite vaulting.

that was devoured by birds and that fell on stony ground and the seed fallen among thorns (which look like neat Victorian posies), both delightfully fresh designs. Slightly later is the particularly fine east window of the Corona—a summary of the theological windows of which the centre panels relate the Passion and Triumph of Christ. The twenty or so side panels, which form the glosses, are astonishing for the elaborate relationships so typical of the medieval passion for synthesis.

The other unusual series are the 12 miracle windows of the Trinity Chapel. Nine of these have survived and are largely filled with ancient glass. They relate the miracles that occurred through the intercession of St Thomas of Canterbury or through the healing virtues of his blood spilt at his murder; the curing of Petronilla the nun of epilepsy; Robert Cricklade, Prior of St Frideswide, of swollen feet; Audrey of Canterbury of quartan fever; Stephen Hoylake of nightmares and so on. Throughout the series, there is a remarkable unity of style, enriched by the geometrical variation in the design of the armatures and the different qualities of the blues.

The remaining glass of the nave and transepts is so scattered and rearranged that it is only worth mentioning that the great west window (dating from the late 14th to mid-15th century) was originally filled with a series of English kings and possibly archbishops. These have now been largely replaced by the genealogical figures from the choir clerestory and the 15th-century tracery lights from the nave, both of which are repeated in the big window in the south-west transept. Its twin in the north-west transept, the Royal Window, was probably ordered by Edward IV in 1465 and originally depicted the 'Seven Glorious Appearances of the Virgin'. Below is represented the royal family adoring the Crucifix, which, with numerous coats of arms, is all that survives.

Figures of the kings of England appear again in the carving of the pulpitum. Indeed, the emphasis on royalty is much more noticeable here than on the continent. All in all, its historical associations played an important part in the story of Canterbury, whose tomb-encrusted walls recall Westminster Abbey and whose glass was protected by sentiment from 18th-century 'improvements'. But of greater significance is the reluctance of the chapter so rich in revenue to bring the eastern parts of the cathedral up to date. Thus there still exist the dramatic flights of stairs connecting storey with storey, which for centuries bore pilgrims to the marble columns and jewelled windows that once surrounded the shrine of St Thomas.

The bottom medallion from Window V from the Trinity Chapel relating the miraculous cure through St Thomas à Becket of the dying cellarer Hugh of Jervaulx. In the lowest petal, Hugh gives thanks at Thomas's shrine.

ESTRECVIVS VESTIS PERO
CVRSIE VESTIS PERO

three (again square-ended) chapels projected. (All these features reappeared in the new 13th-century cathedral.) At the centre of the encampment was a royal fortress, at which in 1086 William the Conqueror assembled his barons for a renewed pledge of fealty. There was constant antagonism and altercation between the castle and the cathedral, which provided a further incentive for moving. It is not surprising, then, that the poet Henry of Avranches wrote in extravagant terms of the new site in the meadows, with its lilies, roses and violets, and the many springs clearer than crystal, purer than gold and softer than ambrosia.

Foundation stones were laid by Bishop Poore in 1220, one for the pope, one for Archbishop Stephen Langton and one for himself. Two more were also laid by William Longspee, half-brother of King John, for himself and his wife. In 1225 the Lady Chapel and two other altars were consecrated. Work must then have proceeded rapidly, for by 1258 the two transepts, the choir and the nave were complete and the cathedral consecrated. Even so, Salisbury's history contains the usual stories of financial embarrassment, for in 1244 an indulgence was granted to all contributors to the cathedral funds. The designer of Salisbury is still conjectural. Nicholas of Ely is described as the master-mason; it seems that the canon, Elias of Dereham, may also have been closely connected with the building work, since he was in charge of the king's works at Winchester and is described as a craftsman in connection with the shrine of St Thomas.

Considerable building took place after the consecration. An unfortunate screen across the west front, designed by Richard Mason, was completed in 1266; and at the end of the century, the cloisters and chapter house (started in 1263) were completed. At this time an impressive bell tower was also erected. This second burst was followed by a pause; then in 1334, a tower and spire were added by Richard Farleigh in a style that completed the increasing magnificence of the chapter house and cloisters.

After the exterior, the interior of Salisbury comes as a slight disappointment. Cool, balanced and remote, it lacks the mesh of rich patterning found in the nave of Lincoln and the warmth and welcome of the golden stone and figured capitals of Wells—both built at the same time in the Early English style. At Salisbury, there is a feeling of austerity; there is no wall arcading, the vaulting is classically quadripartite and all terminations are square and uncompromising.

The landscape of Salisbury Cathedral, opposite, painted by Constable for his friend Bishop Fisher (depicted on the left with his wife) is a superb balance of nature with architecture. Yet the rugged elms and boisterous sky set off magnificently the enduring grace of the Gothic forms.

Carved in Doulting stone and originally coloured and gilded, the remarkable life-like effigy, below, is of William Longspee (died 1226), who was present at the cathedral's foundation.

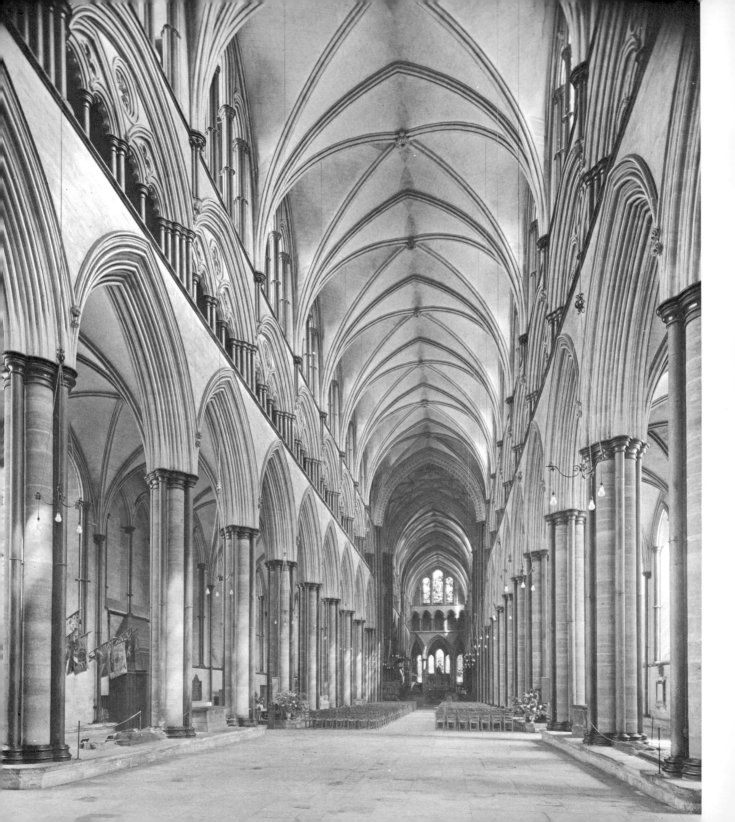

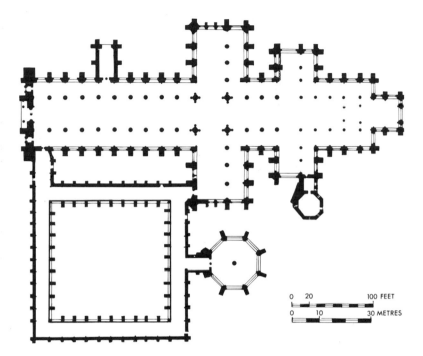

Opposite, the cool and academic interior of Salisbury is almost without figure sculpture; it is also remarkable for its balance of horizontal and vertical.

The plan, left, reflects the uniformity of the cathedral—a series of rectangular compartments —made possible by its virgin site and rapid construction.

Below, some of the magnificent Purbeck piers, all that remain of the original embellishments, which included gilded mouldings and red walls decorated with a delicate scroll in black.

0	20	100 FEET
0	10	30 METRES

The proportions are simple and easily appreciated. The width of the nave and aisles and the height of the vault are equal, and the width of the aisles is about half that of the nave. The length of the main transept, north to south, is the same as the length of the nave; similarly the length of the choir transept roughly equals that of the eastern arm—that is, from the main crossing to the east and excluding the Lady Chapel. The balance of vertical and horizontal is also impressive. The loftiness, the profuse Purbeck shafting and the lancet windows (which are even 'stepped' in the clerestory) are counteracted by the strong horizontals of the circular abaci of the capitals, of the cornice of the main arcade uninterrupted by vaulting shafts, and of the squat gallery with its depressed arches.

Yet in spite of its apparent plainness, Salisbury has its own refinements and riches. The roll mouldings have fillets and are bold and deeply undercut, all features that are multiplied many times in the arches of the arcade and gallery. The stiff-leaf foliage of the period is sparingly used (it is found mostly in the west porches, in the capitals of the retrochoir and in some bosses) as is the 'dogtooth' ornament; on the other hand, there is a profusion of rich and glossy Purbeck

Left, the 'Lady Chapel'—an exquisite example of the Early English style—which originally housed the shrine of St Osmund. Its narrow lancets, steep vaults and monolithic piers are counteracted by an airy breadth.

Right, part of the original choir screen (c. 1260), which once contained statues of kings. The fresh unfurling foliage, garland of musician angels and portrait heads as crisp as antique cameos made it a work of exceptional quality.

marble, varying in colour from a grey-green to a dark brown. Its use in England (inspired perhaps by accounts of the rich marbled interiors brought back by returning crusaders) was introduced at Canterbury. It quickly gained popularity and is considered one of the hallmarks of the Early English style.

The most unusual part of the 13th-century cathedral is the lovely Lady Chapel, the earliest part of the building. It had a particular sanctity since it housed the bodies of three bishops including St Osmund, whose rich stone shrine was placed in the centre of the chapel. Slender lancet windows, a steep pitch to the vault, and attenuated piers in monoliths of Purbeck marble combine with the

equal height of aisles and nave to create an impression of airy breadth. This hall treatment is rare at such an early date. A portion of the choir screen is another exquisite example of 13th-century work. In the niches were statues of kings and above was a gallery from which the Gospel was read on certain days. Its many individual heads and the lush, unfurling foliage reflects a new interest in nature, which is striking when compared with the earlier abstract motifs of the stiff-leaf and dogtooth ornament.

Walking round the cathedral, one notices various remedial measures made necessary by the erection of the spire in the 14th century. This was on a far more ambitious scale than anything attempted by the 13th-century masons. The piers, each only six foot square, were not strong enough to support the 6400 tons

The simple and pleasing motif of a reversed arch was used to strengthen the choir transepts after the erection of the spire. As seen in the view, opposite, they provide a dramatic perspective.

Below, the cloisters of Salisbury (1263–84), the largest and earliest remaining example; they are distinguished for their bold geometrical tracery, open on one side and repeated in blind form on the other.

Above, part of the unique Old Testament frieze of sculpture in the chapter house, depicting the drunkenness of Noah and the building of the Ark.

The spacious octagonal chapter house, opposite, was built for a chapter that was noted for its learning. It is modelled on that of Westminster with fine geometrical tracery and stained glass (all replaced).

Left, a view of the chapter house vault, whose lucid design is based on pure geometry. An inverted cone fans out its 16 ribs to meet the 24 springing from the 8 corners.

147

of masonry, and flying buttresses were immediately added to transmit the weight from the clerestory walls down to the outer walls of the aisles; further internal buttresses were also added, partly hidden inside the gallery. A decade or so later, reversed arches were inserted in the opening of the choir transepts. These are similar in design to the magnificent strainer arches of Wells; they are not so powerful a feature, however, although a dramatic perspective can be obtained by looking laterally across the transepts. Next are the heavy Perpendicular arches inserted by Bishop Beauchamp at the beginning of the 15th century to reinforce the piers of the main crossing. Similar in design to those of Canterbury inserted after the erection of Bell Harry Tower, they are unpleasantly coarse and scaled up in detail. Towards the end of the 15th century, a lierne vault was added underneath the steeple, as was common practice at the time; this strengthened the area and created a ceiling to what was originally a lantern tower. The bulge towards the top of the Purbeck shafts of the north-west pier at the crossing testifies how necessary this reinforcement was.

Off the south-west corner of the south transept are the cloisters, presided over aptly by the cedar tree. Built from about 1263 onwards by Richard Mason, they are the earliest surviving example of a complete cloister; they are also the largest and one of the most magnificent. The walks, each as long as the nave, are designed in the enriched forms of the Early English style; this consists of a four-lighted window with a handsome deeply moulded motif of a cinquefoiled circle in the head—a pattern of strength and sinew compared with the inset plate tracery of the gallery. A blind version of the design is repeated on the inner walls, above which the ribs are extended to form a quadripartite vault.

The west front was also designed by Richard Mason, his first work on the cathedral. After the coherent design of the work that precedes it, it shows an embarrassing lack of co-ordination both internally, between the inside west wall and the elevation of the aisles, and externally, where the lateral buttresses mask any possible relationship with the building behind. Moreover its seven storeys of blind arcading, figured niches, sunk quatrefoils and porches have nothing in common with the interior, a simple triple-aisled vessel of only three storeys. Screen fronts are an English speciality, Anglo-Norman in origin, and were a form of public reredos, undoubtedly enriched with colour and crowded with witnessing saints. At Salisbury, these figures were restored by Redfern in 1862; only

Right, a view of the cathedral from the south-west showing how the extensive layout is pulled together by Richard Farleigh's magnificent spire (1334–65), which rises like a flowering shoot from the elementary early English forms to the record height in England of 404 feet.

The importance of timberwork in medieval building is reflected in the view, below, inside the spire showing the original scaffolding.

St Peter and St Paul to the left and right of the great west window and four other saints are original.

If there are reservations about the west front, the tower and spire have always been universally acclaimed. Built by Richard Farleigh, the tower provides the important centralising unit to the 13th-century building, which was in any case probably meant to have a lantern tower, though perhaps with only a much shorter spire out of wood. The decorative motifs applied on the exterior are also beautifully integrated with the earlier building, the lancets echoed in the slender traceried windows and the blind arcading of the eaves translated into canopied string courses carved with filigree precision; here the earlier dogtooth becomes the ballflower of the Decorated period. Finally, the many elementary pinnacles of the 13th-century cathedral are echoed in the four more complex extensions of the corner buttresses. Inserted in the angles between the tower and the octagonal form of the steeple are four additional pinnacles of great delicacy, which prepare for the final magnificent leap. Like so many feats of medieval building, the spire involved calculations that were within a hair's breadth of safety or disaster. At Salisbury, the spire has a long history of constant supervision. Apart from the measures already described, the spire was strengthened by Wren (whose recommendations can be seen in the library) and later by George Gilbert Scott, this time with iron supports and ties. Finally in 1950, rusting combined with weathering made it necessary to rebuild the top 30 feet. The original wooden scaffolding round which the spire was built has never been removed and the old wooden windlass used for raising the material is still in use.

During the building of the spire, two sides of the close were walled in. The other two sides are enclosed by the river. The houses that surround the close present a fascinating sample of some outstanding English domestic architecture. Many of the buildings today house colleges of education, thus continuing Salisbury's ancient tradition of learning. The spacious and secluded close is of course a legacy from the numerous monastic precincts of Norman times, and represents an essential part of the character of an English cathedral. Indeed, Salisbury has all the other ingredients—square ends, separate compartments, important cloisters, a notable chapter house, and an emphasis on length. But its particular virtue is the homogeneity of its style. The arid, Early English details in the main body develop into a rich traceried design in the cloisters and chapter house, with the 14th-century steeple as the final flowering shoot.

CHAPTER 10

ELY

Situated on what was once an island, Ely Cathedral overlooks the surrounding stretches of the fens—a haunting and mysterious silhouette. It is also the dominating presence of the town, which is no more than a fringe around the monastic precincts on the south side, tails off on the east down back alleys to the river, and on the north is only two to three streets wide; only on the west are there buildings in any substance. The relationship of cathedral to town can have altered little since the middle ages; here, then, is a rare example of a medieval cathedral in its original setting.

The conventional view of the cathedral reveals a typical Anglo-Norman silhouette of immense length, divided at intervals by the vertical forms of buttresses, pinnacles and towers. With the towers is introduced the characteristic peculiar to Ely—the predominance of polygonal forms. Instead of the usual rectangular forms of Norman origin, completed or heightened in the Perpendicular period, the Norman turrets of the eastern transept are eight-sided, those of the later western transept, ten-sided, and when the Norman tower over the central crossing collapsed in 1322, it was replaced by the famous Octagon. (It is tempting to wonder whether these earlier turrets may have been partly responsible for the designer's choice of this form.) A further lantern added at the top of the central tower of the west end at the end of the 14th century repeats the octagonal form of the Octagon, built with four long sides and four short. A further modification of angular forms appears in the flowing curves and double curves in ogee form of the Decorated tracery found in the choir windows, in the Octagon and, most conspicuously and sumptuously, in the windows of the Lady Chapel.

Further forms of decoration appear in the unusually rich arcading

covering the western frontispiece. Carried out in the last decades of the 12th century, at a time when in France the Gothic style had been established for more than a generation and the choir at Canterbury was being rebuilt also in this style, the Anglo-Norman here is rather in the nature of a swansong. Above a plain plinth to give stability is an arcade of extremely narrow arches surmounted by one of wider arches in two layers; then comes a tier of alternating narrow and wide arches (the latter glazed), of which the supporting shafts are stepped and the orders decorated with zigzag and billet motifs, while the wall is ornamented with a shingle pattern. Above this is a row of corbel heads and more trefoil-headed arches enclosing round-headed arches also stepped back and decorated with zigzags. Above this is another glazed storey, Transitional in style, with sunk quatre-foils and shaft-rings, and terminating in pierced crenellations on the skyline. The turrets, which are also Transitional with pointed arches, themselves continue for another three storeys, of which the first is glazed and the third open, adding a quality of lift essential to the upper stages of a tower. The shafts are a curious feature; at the stage or storey of the trefoil arches they are reduced to one for each facet and, instead of emphasising the corners, run through the middle cutting in front of each window.

But the most striking feature of this western frontispiece is the design. One superb central tower replaces the usual twin towers of Norman design, flanked on either side by a pair of smaller towers (the northern tower collapsed in the 15th century). Remains at Bury St Edmunds suggest a similar design, though these are later in date. A more direct source would seem to lie in the earlier Anglo-Saxon church which, according to contemporary chronicles, had a western transept; other Fenland monasteries, refounded like Ely in the 10th century, also had single western towers.

The first foundation at Ely was established in 673 by St Ethelreda and it may, as was the custom of the time, have housed a joint order of monks and nuns. A hundred years later, a reform movement in the Benedictine order, initiated in England by St Dunstan, built a new monastery. It was modest in size, but as powerful as the two great Wessex monasteries of Winchester and Glastonbury; it was also famous for its scriptorium. It became the headquarters of Here-ward the Wake during his resistance to William the Conqueror. Apart from illuminated manuscripts, nothing survives from this time.

The third (and existing) building was founded by Abbot Simeon, a kinsman of William the Conqueror and brother of Bishop Walkelin

Above, a view showing the textured patterning like a giant Aran stitch, which covers the impressive late Norman south-west transept. (The north-west arm collapsed in the 15th century.)

Opposite, an aerial view of Ely Cathedral. Until 1836 it was the seat of both temporal and spiritual power wielded by the bishop; even today it is the dominant feature of the small town of Ely and the surrounding Fens.

153

of Winchester. It was begun in 1083 and by 1106 the choir and central tower had been completed and the relics of St Ethelreda translated. (In 1109 Ely was made into a see, of which the bishop was also the abbot. In addition, he was in charge of civil jurisdiction, as at Durham, in order that he might guard against any future outbreaks from this last remaining pocket of Anglo-Saxon resistance.) Meantime, from 1090 onwards, work proceeded on the transepts and the lengthy nave of 13 bays, which was finished by 1130. After a pause lasting a generation, the western transepts were added and the impressive single tower built at the west end. The next enterprise, between 1239 and 1250, involved the extension eastwards of the choir, in order to provide a more sumptuous setting for the shrine of St Ethelreda and more space for visiting pilgrims. At the same time, a western porch or Galilee was added. The cathedral now lacked only a Lady Chapel, whose foundations were laid in 1321. The following year, however, the central tower collapsed, destroying with it the western bays of the choir. The crossing was then rebuilt in its famous octagonal form and covered with the vault and lantern in wood, which were finished by 1346. At the base of the hood moulds of the smaller arches of the Octagon are heads that are probably portraits of the men responsible for the Octagon's construction—the sacrist Alan of Walsingham, his two successive master-masons (both called John), Prior Crauden, Bishop Hotham and the king's carpenter, William Hurley. At the same time the ruined bays of the choir were rebuilt and work was resumed on the Lady Chapel. Also belonging to this creative period is the entrancing private chapel of Prior Crauden (now used by King's School) and the choir stalls (built between 1336–48), which were originally placed in the central crossing.

After the Black Death only minor additions were made, including a lantern on the west tower at the end of the 14th century and the handsome gatehouse known as the Ely Porta. Finally, the end bays of the choir aisles were converted into two remarkable chantry chapels. The first is that of Bishop Alcock (1488–1500) on the north, built in a style that continued the canopies of the 14th-century stalls—a tight profusion of crockets, niches and lacy undercutting carved in a very soft local limestone; the other is that of Bishop West (1523–36) on the south, in which the net vault was decorated with exquisite Renaissance motifs in a perfect blending of the two cultures. At the end of the 17th century, a new doorway was made into the west aisle of the north transept in a design (similar to that

154

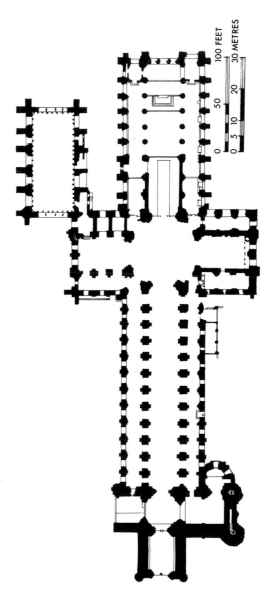

Peculiar features of the plan of Ely are the Anglo-Norman western transepts dominated by a central tower and flanked by pairs of smaller ones; the curious siting of the Lady Chapel off the north-west transept; and the unique opening out of the central crossing in the 14th century.

of the imposing door of St Mary-le-Bow) which was carried out by a mason of Christopher Wren, whose uncle Dr Mathew was bishop of Ely.

The appearance of the interior is more consistent than might be expected from its long history of rebuilding and embellishment. The late Anglo-Norman western transept, although coldly and correctly restored during the 19th century, has tall and narrow proportions similar to those of the nave and is decorated with the same vocabulary of motifs but in an accelerated rhythm; the same is true of the eastern transepts, but because these are the earliest surviving parts (the south-eastern is the earlier) the rhythm is much slower. Here unmoulded orders appear in the arcade and only every alternate bay is articulated with a demi-shaft in a design that follows the transepts of Winchester built by Bishop Walkelin. Even the rich Gothic of the east end, although different in appearance, uses the same length of bay and divisions within the bay and similar proportions to those of the storeys.

This uniformity was the result of two successive adjustments in rebuilding; everywhere else at this time clerestories were growing larger and galleries were shrinking to a nominal triforium. The choir's major differences are the loftier arcade, the more slender piers and the more obtuse pitch of the vault, all of which create a new feeling of spaciousness that is enhanced by the stepped design of parallel lancets comprising the east window. And finally there is a whole summertime of vegetation. Even though a century lies between the later three bays of the chancel and the earlier six of the presbytery, they are similar in style. The presbytery is Early English, which in addition to Purbeck marble shafting and dogtooth ornament and stiff-leaf capitals delights in a scalloped cusping to the arches and a multiplication of ribs in the vaulting as well as profuse foliage in the brackets supporting the vaulting shafts. This is the style found in the porch of the Galilee and is characteristic of the final stage of this style weakened by over-enrichment and lack of new forms. By the time the chancel was rebuilt, tracery had been introduced into the Gothic style and the windows of both clerestory and gallery are rich with the flowing forms of the Decorated style, although here they are curiously lax. The star pattern of the vault—the earliest existing example of its type—is crisp and delicate in comparison.

To return to the nave and to walk down the twelve successive bays of bare scaffolding is like plunging into midwinter. The nave at Ely is roughly contemporary with that of Durham, but without its

The presbytery, built in 1239–52 as a sumptuous setting for the shrine of St Ethelreda, used scalloped cusping, sheafed vaulting ribs and a profusion of Purbeck shafting and stiff-leaf foliage.

155

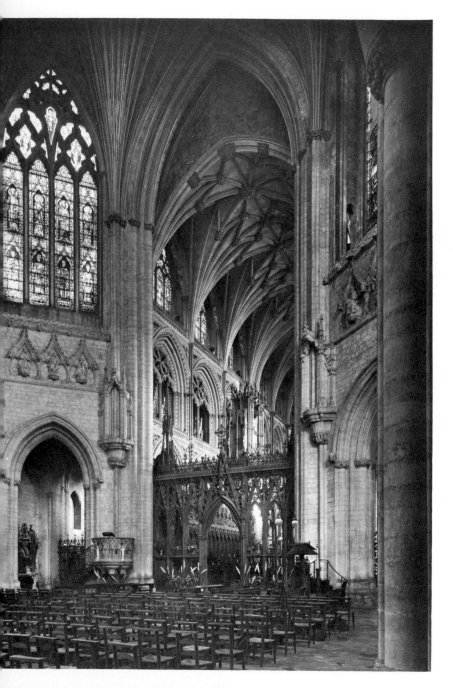

A sense of spaciousness is conveyed by the view, left, of three sides of the Octagon carved out of the central crossing after the collapse of the tower in 1322. Also contemporary are the three lower-pitched choir bays with their flowing tracery and star-patterned vault.

Right, a view from the Octagon along the tunnel of the nave showing its 12 bays of bare scaffolding rising to a height of 86 feet.

A strong sense of decoration and of dynamic movement appear in the flat carving of the Prior's door (c. 1140), far right. On the tympanum is carved Christ in Glory, borne by ecstatic angels (a rare subject in English sculpture).

spacious proportions and stimulating design or the upward lift of its lofty arcade and ribbed vault. At Ely each storey is about the same size, the alternation of bays in scarcely noticeable and the overhead covering a wooden ceiling, painted in the 19th century. The nave of Ely, at 86 feet high, is taller than any other existing Norman nave; it is also narrower, or as narrow. But the most important characteristic of its design is the balance of void and solid. Even Laon, more than a century later, failed to open up the wall any more. Originally, the nave would have had a less tunnel-like feeling, for a Norman screen the height of the arcade stood between the third pair of piers from the crossing—that is, one bay to the west of the Monk's Door.

Luckily, this doorway and the even more remarkable Prior's door further west have both survived and provide examples of some of the richest English sculpture of this century. Subject-matter and style are both unusual, and show a curious blend from many sources. On the jambs of the Prior's door are varieties of foliage scroll inhabited by men and beasts similar to those of northern Italy. The subject of the tympanum, Christ in Glory, is also un-English though the flat and linear technique shows the influence of English manuscript illuminations, and its abstract vitality of line is a legacy inherited from Viking art.

All that was built up to this period was not so different from the general run of Anglo-Norman cathedrals. This was transformed by the Octagon. The collapse of the central tower on February 22, 1322, ruined the first three bays of the choir and damaged the nearest bay of each of the other three arms. The replacement of the old box lantern with the new enlarged octagonal form was therefore a practical expedient; nevertheless it was a revolutionary conception. There had been several earlier polygonal buildings: chapter houses for instance, of which that at York (c. 1285) covered a span of 58 feet without a central pier and was even vaulted in wood. At Ely, however, this form was used for the Octagon—the culminating feature of the cathedral, which crowns the central crossing with the importance of a dome.

The lantern of Ely is made of wood; the span of 70 feet was too wide for a stone vault. Built on the principle of the hammer-beam (of which it is perhaps the earliest example), the horizontal and the lower diagonal beams are angled into the corners of the masonry Octagon, which is reinforced by pinnacles and flying buttresses. Above these beams rises the lantern, lit by traceried windows, and

The Octagon, left, opens out of the nave, choir and transepts like the joyous burst of a dome. Seventy feet are spanned by eight cones of ribbed vaulting, which rise to meet the octagonal lantern—Alan of Walsingham's ingenious and delicate design executed entirely in wood.

Below, a model of the Octagon and lantern showing the main structural timbers. By means of horizontal hammer-beams and further diagonal beams (64 × 9 feet), the Octagon is angled into the eight corners of the stone tower.

A grid of vaulting shafts, mullions and canopied panels define the structure of the remarkable Lady Chapel, above (built in the 1330s), while its sense of space is enhanced by the motif of the nodding ogee arch.

Left, part of the nodding ogee arcade carved out of a local chalk along the sides of the Lady Chapel; its undulating vegetation again expresses the new sensibility to space.

Silhouetted like a crown against the Fens, the Octagon, right, with its storeyed towers and traceried windows transforms the Norman pile of Ely into a fairy-tale castle.

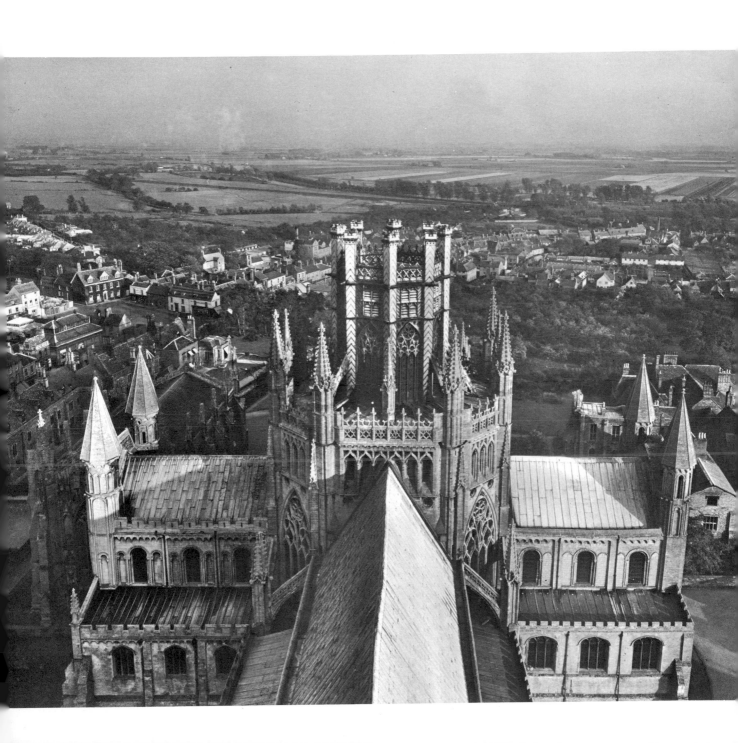

over the eight-pointed star of the ceiling is the belfry. From below the structural hammer-beams are not visible, since they are lined by the cones of ribbed vaulting, also of wood, which spring from the capitals of the crossing piers to join the eight sides at the bottom of the lantern. The highly functional nature of this feat of engineering blends well with the structural purity of the surrounding Norman architecture. Only the Decorated tracery of the four 'clerestory' windows, echoed in the little ogee arcade of the triforium and the tabernacles below, add a period flavour. But even here a concession to the earlier style had been made by the empty surfaces and the thickness of the tracery.

After the Octagon anything but the Lady Chapel would be an anticlimax. First, there is the same sense of space, showing an emphasis on width as opposed to height. Then the motif of the little ogee arcade of the Octagon has been expanded into an elaborate design of canopied niches consisting of 'nodding' ogee arches cusped with further ogees. Formed into seats, the niches line the walls as in a chapter house. The canopies above are covered in a riot of vegetation reminiscent of diseased oak or bladderwrack seaweed, the surface seething and bubbling in the same way as, on a larger scale, the arcade undulates in and out of the central area. The general effect would be restless without the vertical structure of canopied panels enclosing the buttresses between the windows, which are echoed in the panelled tracery of the east window and reinforced by the mullions of the other windows. This vertical emphasis is further stressed by the vaulting shafts, which pass behind the nodding niches. This motif is also found in the tabernacles in the corners of the Octagon and is another example of the new interest in penetrating space. Traces of gilding and colour on the niches in the north-east corner and fragments of glass in the opposite window (suggesting a design of canopied figures incorporating some white glass and silver stain) indicate that the original appearance of the chapel must have been far richer and more sombre. There also ran a narrative of the life of the Virgin and her miracles between the gables of the arcade. This was carved out of a soft local limestone, but is sadly mutilated; only a few exquisite fragments remain.

No staggering conclusions can be drawn from Ely. It was neither the first nor the best in any field. Its main achievement lies in the union, rather than juxtaposition, of two disparate styles. This fusion is perhaps most happily realised in the towering and turreted fantasy seen from across the river.

The medieval passion for geometry created the breath-taking purity of this octagon vault executed by the most distinguished carpenter of the day, William Hurle. Note the twist to the setting of the two stars, a structural as well as a decorative feature.

do not convey the same impression of sap rising in a growing plant. Forms tend to lose their sense of structural logic; in the enclosing arch of the principal rose, the supporting shafts have shrivelled to nominal supports, and in the probably more recent arches puncturing some of the outer walls at ground level, they have been dispensed with altogether. The gallery of the west front enclosing the kings of Castile is a two-dimensional inset only loosely corresponding to the windows below and unrelated to the design of the flanking towers. The equivalent feature above the transepts is even more patently a two-dimensional screen.

The decoration is precise, meticulous and mathematical. Knobs—for they are no longer crockets—succeed one another with mechanical regularity up the openings of the tower windows. Gothic lettering replaces or is combined with Flamboyant tracery in the decoration of the parapets, although its general treatment and even the emphasis are so abstract that at first glance it fails to stand out as a foreign element. (This lettering was among the many features at Burgos that provided Gaudi with his rich store of forms for the Sagrada Familia at Barcelona.) The original inspiration for this decorative richness is of course the Islamic culture of Spain, which reached its peak at Cordova and Seville between the eighth and 12th centuries, when they were perhaps the most civilised cities in Europe. Without the decorative additions, mostly of the 15th and 16th centuries, Burgos Cathedral would be unremarkable.

Opposite, a view showing how massive and extensive outbuildings pile up towards the elaborate central cimborio. Note the imposing screen top to the transept front and the juxtaposition of plain and ornate surfaces.

Left, a panoramic view of the cathedral, whose spires and pinnacles were created by three generations of the Colonia family. Hans of Cologne (Colonia) built those of the façade (on the right); his son Simon those of the Constable's Chapel (on the left); and his grandson Francisco those of the central crossing. 167

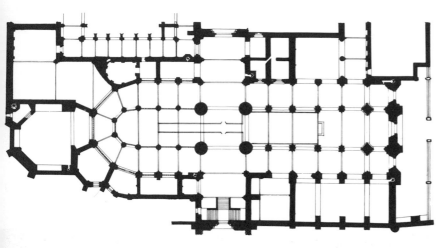

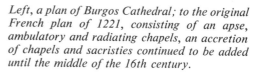

Left, a plan of Burgos Cathedral; to the original French plan of 1221, consisting of an apse, ambulatory and radiating chapels, an accretion of chapels and sacristies continued to be added until the middle of the 16th century.

Below, a view of the Constable's Chapel. Here exotic decoration combines with the pure geometry of the architecture to make the chapel the epitome of Burgos.

The cathedral was founded in 1221, at a time when a wave of interest in European culture north of the Pyrenees led to the building of the 'French' cathedrals of Toledo and León. King Ferdinand III (later canonised) laid the foundation stone in the presence of Bishop Mauricio, who had studied in Paris and travelled extensively in Europe. The first master-mason was one Ricardo, a protégé of the English Queen Eleanor of Castile. In 1243 Ricardo died and work was taken over by the master-mason Enrique, probably a Frenchman who had also worked at León. He completed the transepts and nave by 1260—a rate of building as speedy as that of any Ile de France cathedral—and in the same style. Thirty years later it was decided to build cloisters—a feature found in most Spanish cathedrals despite their secular foundation. The mason at this time was probably a Spaniard, Juan Perez, who also designed the chapter house or Chapel of Santa Catalina. So far the building was in the French High Gothic tradition, with flying buttresses, elementary tracery and stained glass, sculptured portals and radiating chapels. Its many-pinnacled silhouette is the product of the period between the mid-15th century and the mid-16th. First, the two magnificent western steeples were erected by the master-mason Hans of Cologne (Juan de

Colonia to the Spaniards), followed between 1482–94 by the Chapel

of the Constable designed by his Spanish-born son Simon de Colonia. Finally, between 1540–68, his grandson Francisco built the central *cimborio* (lantern) replacing that of Juan, which had been famed for its beauty but had collapsed.

At this time Burgos had developed into a prosperous international trading centre with a population of over 80,000 and a navy that plied from ports on the north coast of Spain. It also had a distinguished and battle-scarred history. According to tradition, it was founded by Diego Porcelos, who in 882 had repopulated this outpost on the frontier between Arab and Christian Spain and set a castle on its promontory. Arab raids continued, however, throughout the ninth century, and Burgos did not achieve any measure of sovereignty over other Castilian towns until 950. In this year Fernan Gonzalez became the first count and in 1035 his great-grandson Ferdinand the first king of Castile, to which he added by his marriage the kingdom of León. At this time too, in 1075, the see was transferred from Oca to Burgos, although no cathedral had yet been started. Perhaps this proud history inspired the cathedral's eventual image of a pinnacled castle. Certainly the silhouette of Burgos is unparalleled in Spain, where cathedrals are usually topped with towers and domes.

On turning to the interior, we find that the same rich effect has

been created during this late medieval period of prosperity. The impact of the grandeur and opulence is immediate and overwhelming. Only three bays from the west end the towering forged-iron grille of the late 15th-century *coro* (choir) rises well above the height of the arcade, completely enclosing the three remaining bays of the nave in its awe-inspiring veiling. It continues after the transepts, railing in the three bays of the choir and the Capilla Mayor, and thus providing an undisturbed processional way from the High Altar into the nave—that is, more than half the total length of the cathedral. No pulpitum or choir screen in the cathedrals of other countries can match the majesty and mystery of these Spanish screens or *rejas*, enriched with architectural motifs, heraldic display and religious figures. Here screens partition off each chapel of the ambulatory including the vast Chapel of the Constable. In every direction (except to the west) extensions are formed by chapels, sacristies, treasuries, cloisters and chapter house, loosely and asymmetrically connected by further screens to the central body. Area, rather than height as in France or length as in England, is the governing factor in Spain.

Our attention is next attracted by the towering altarpieces. (Although this type is not peculiar to Spain, it is a particularly popular feature and the city of Burgos is rich in fine examples.) The altarpiece or *retablo* of the High Altar, carved by various artists between 1562–80 in the High Renaissance style, consists of four storeys of niches, each occupied by heroic figures and crowned by further figures silhouetted against the clerestory windows of the apse. In the Chapel of St Anna off the north aisle of the nave next to the transept is another *retablo* occupying an entire wall. This is by Gil de Siloe from Nuremberg and Diego de la Cruz; it is carved with fantastic feats of undercutting and painted in blue and gold suggesting a precious *champlevé* enamel. This style, usually termed Early or Isabelline Plateresque, was created by a society revelling in the first influx of silver and gold from the recently discovered New World. A further enormous *retablo*, carved between 1523–6 by the Burgundian Felipe de Vigarni and the famous architect and sculptor Diego de Siloe (the son of Gil) is in the Chapel of the Constable. It is in the style known as Later Plateresque and combines heroic figures, which are Northern in their realism, with a decorative repertoire of Renaissance and even Moorish motifs. (This often unattractive amalgam was often found in Northern Europe at this time, where the new spirit of the Italian Renaissance had not yet been digested.)

Slightly earlier in date, also by Felipe de Vigarni together with

Above, the star-patterned vault of the crossing, the most intricate at Burgos. Here, in two layers containing a variety of geometrical design, all sense of structure has been replaced by a passion for pattern-making of Islamic inspiration.

Opposite, the vault of the Constable's Chapel, which, like the petals and stamens of a flower, combines the play of plain and ornamented surfaces, enriched by a further layer of stained glass through the tracery. 171

Andres de Najera, are the hundred-odd sumptuous choir stalls in the same style, but here incorporating on the seats designs of box inlay. Also by Felipe de Vigarni but pure Gothic in feeling are three exquisite reliefs in the Trassagrario, the screen surrounding the choir. The impression of richness and grandeur is further increased by the imposing lecterns, the illuminated choir books, the priceless treasures of the several sacristies, and the many paintings and works of art displayed in the chapels, each of which is a museum in itself. The most venerated chapel is that of the Santissimo Christo, in which there is a figure of the crucified Christ with articulated limbs carved out of wood and covered with leather, allegedly the work of Nicodemus.

A more integral part of the architecture are the many lovely star-patterned vaults, which are a characteristic feature of Burgalese Gothic. The earliest, in the Chapel of the Visitation, was probably designed by Juan de Colonia in the mid-15th century. Slightly later is the vault of the Constable's Chapel—a miracle of purity and delicacy by Simon de Colonia. Here the plain panels of the star pattern contrast with the rich concentration of open tracery at its centre. An even later variation appears in the Chapel of the Presentation and another in the Chapel of Santa Catalina. Indeed, almost every chapel has a lierne vault with a star pattern of some kind. The true Burgalese type re-appears in the remarkable mid-16th century vault over the *cimborio*, which consists of an even richer variety of intricate geometrical patterns, even more closely related to Islamic fretwork, the continuing source of all these examples. And in them, all sense of vault structure is now quite gone.

Under the accretions of three centuries, the bare bones of the original structure can still be detected. Essentially it is based on various examples of French High Gothic. The plan of the choir resembles that of Coutances, although uncertainty in dating suggests that the choir of the Cistercian foundation at Pontigny was a possible source in common. The elevation recalls Bourges, with its shafts rising from floor to vault, the design of the triforium and a curious detail in the cusped circular openings in the vaulting compartments of the apse. Even so there are significant differences. The triforium at Bourges has a sense of 'lift' and feeling for structure that is absent from Burgos. Burgos on the other hand does not so much open up the wall as throw over it a screen of decoration, which later generations felt impelled to embellish further with balustrades of Flamboyant tracery and arcs of corbel heads. In the tracery of the windows, the

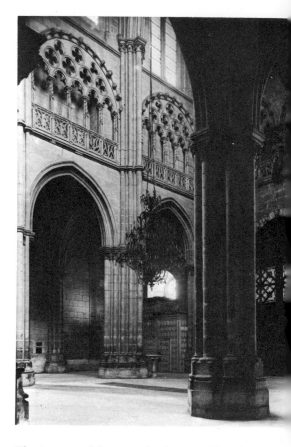

The interior of Burgos closely resembles that of Bourges in its uninterrupted shafts and the design of its triforium. Yet there is not the same sense of lift, and surface decoration is preferred to an emphasis on structure.

master-mason was no doubt thinking of the recently designed windows of Reims. Similarly the magnificent design of the transept fronts.

The portals also derive from the Ile de France. That on the south side, the Puerta del Sarmental, is the earlier, dating between 1228–30. On the tympanum Christ and the evangelists are represented in an unusual way: Christ is depicted not in glory, as on the Portail Royal of Chartres, but as the Teacher and Preceptor while the evangelists appear as animal symbols from the Book of Revelation and in human form as the authors of the gospels busily occupied at their lecterns—a common scene in Romanesque and earlier manuscripts. The figure on the central doorpost represents Bishop Mauricio (possibly a contemporary portrait) and the later jamb figures Moses, Aaron and Joseph on the left and St Peter and St Paul and an unidentified figure on the right.

Above, the monumental head (c. 1250–1300) of the pretty Violante of Aragon, who stands in the cloister with her husband Alfonso the Wise (the successor to St Ferdinand).

Above left, the Puerta del Sarmental (which derives in type from the Ile de France), crisp, lively and of high quality. It shows Christ as teacher surrounded by the evangelists both as writers of the gospels and in animal form. 173

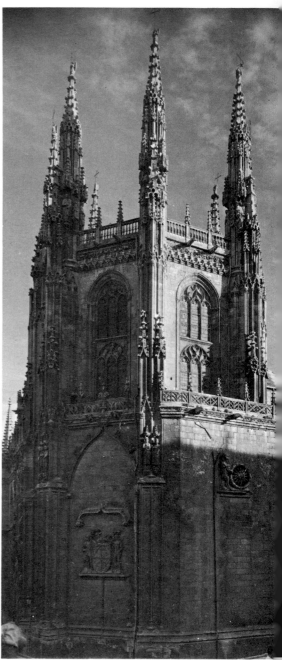

The portal on the north side, the Puerta de la Coroneria, was finished by 1257 and shows the Last Judgement, a somewhat simplified version compared with those of the Ile de France. But it is rich in individual figures of great beauty—for example, the cherubim enveloped in their magnificent wings and the ingenious little scenes of resurrecting figures, all inserted into the voussoirs. According to contemporary documents, the lintel refers to the promulgation of papal bulls of indulgence for the founding of convents—a rare subject in medieval art. The apostles below, strongly antique in appearance, have been compared to figures at Amiens (presumably from the south transept), which, according to Huidobro, the author of the monograph on Burgos, may be the work of the same Italian journeymen. The little portal of the cloisters dates from the turn of the 13th and 14th centuries and reflects the intimacy and graciousness of this period. In the cloisters, characteristically set against a blank wall, are the figures of Alfonso the Wise and Violante of Aragon (who succeeded St Ferdinand), two examples from a group of sturdy upright characters that includes a king at Reims and the two saintly knights of Chartres.

Finally there is the *cimborio* (1539–67) by Francisco de Colonia, decorated by Felipe de Vigarni and completed by Juan de Vallejo.

175

This is a work ebulliently three-dimensional in its detail, which as well as earlier Flamboyant forms includes herm figures, busts full of *Angst* that burst out of their medallions, a frieze of swarming putti and, at three different levels, a balustrade that curves and twists around the octagon. A repertoire of similar motifs decorates the four heavy circular piers and pendentives of the crossing, but here the parade of so much Renaissance ornament, which may be amusing and magnificent in the Escalera Dorada, when incorporated into the architecture of the centre of the church becomes rather repellent in its vulgarity.

The Chapel of the Constable (1482–94—little more than a generation earlier) is equally rich and exuberant, but here the result is totally successful. There is the characteristic Spanish balance of ornamental features set against blank backgrounds: huge shields held by 'wild men' or slung askew in a heraldic setting, which is re-echoed in the stained glass of the clerestory. As the eye travels upwards, the decoration increases in complexity, while decreasing in weight. The doily-like frills that line the niches are as intricate and crisp as filigree ivory, and the stellar vault seems to float above our heads, while through its delicate tracery can be seen a further layer set with glass. Germanic heraldry, Burgundian figurework, Flamboyant tracery, *mudéjar* openwork and an Italian tomb are all included in this masterpiece of Isabelline Plateresque, which is held together by sheer vitality. But its impact and unity is largely the product of the basic octagonal form of the chapel, each side of which is strongly defined by horizontal and vertical lines. Thus the decoration in the Constable's Chapel, unlike that of much of the rest of the cathedral, is part of the structure itself.

The chapel's creator, Simon of Cologne, like all architects of the time, was contributing to the disintegration of form that was becoming a feature of the Gothic style. He was indeed working on the same lines as his father Juan when he designed the western spires, which have been reduced to an open grid in stone, although the earlier pyramidal type can still be seen. His model must have been the spires of the cathedral in his home town, which at the time existed only on paper; they were not erected until the 19th century. The spires of Burgos, each group (as we have seen) the creation of a generation of the remarkable Colonia family, themselves inspired another magnificent church, the Sagrada Familia by Gaudi, which even in its unfinished state holds the promise of becoming one of the greatest buildings of its kind in modern times.

176

Exotic furnishings and ornaments, the pattern of tracery and wrought-iron grilles and the towering forms of the architecture all contribute to the majesty and mystery conveyed in this view of the central crossing of Burgos.

CHAPTER 12

STRASBOURG

Strasbourg is a city of steeply pitched roofs where dormer windows rise in rows to the topmost attics and gables often climb in crowsteps; even the houses are a couple of storeys higher than those in the west. It was therefore inevitable that the cathedral should seek to achieve a particularly impressive height. With the crowning figure of the Virgin the spire finally rose to approximately 480 feet—an unbeaten achievement until Ulm completed its spire in the 19th century and the skyscrapers of New York set up fresh records in our own time.

This emphasis on height is underlined by every element of Strasbourg Cathedral: by the four buttresses, the pair of towers, the mullions of the windows, the gables and finally by the single steeple (the effect would have been halved if there had been two). The impression is reinforced by the screen of arcading that almost covers the entire surface of the façade, frequently doubling the verticals of the building behind but always separated by a gap of two feet. Here lie the nerves of the building, taut and bare.

Compared with the intensity and tension of Strasbourg, Reims (which has a façade of comparable majesty) seems composed and relaxed. Even so, there is much of Reims in Strasbourg. The figures of the Church and the Synagogue appear to be inspired by Reims, while the design of the façade (especially the base with its three gabled portals, linked by blind portals) is to be found in embryo in the French cathedral, which itself derives from the other great church of Reims—St Nicaise, begun in 1231. Finally (and perhaps paradoxically) there is a basic classical harmony present in both façades—the harmony of the High Gothic.

Tradition attributes the site to that occupied by the forum of the Roman town of Argentoratum, on which at least two successive

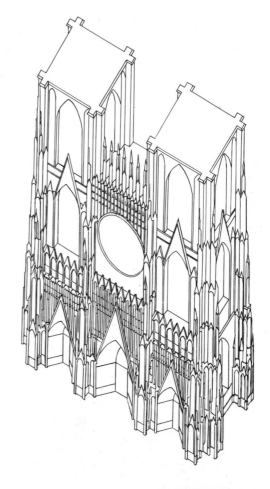

churches arose before the foundation of the present cathedral. The earliest part of the cathedral today is the eastern portion of the crypt comprising an apse, a nave covered by a barrel vault and aisles by groined vaults; alternating piers and columns form the supports. It is decorated with various forms of embellishment—richly carved capitals, keystones of alternating colours in the arches and bands of geometrical designs incised into the walls of the apse. The crypt belonged originally to the church of Bishop Wernher (begun in 1015) on whose foundations the present cathedral stands. As well as the crypt, it consisted of a deep apse, flanked by chapels two storeys high, transepts of the present dimensions and, curiously, no choir. Altogether Wernher's cathedral was of impressive proportions, extending further west than the cathedral of today, and equalled in size only by the vast cathedral of Speyer. Strasbourg at this time was described as the most powerful centre in the German Empire ruled by the Salian Dynasty, which was then at the height of its influence. Indeed German architecture in the first half of the 11th century was the finest in Europe, more magnificent in scale and design than anything produced in France or England.

In 1176 this church was destroyed by fire, and a few years later Bishop Henry I decided to embark on a total reconstruction. Only the foundations of Wernher's building were kept, the walls being thickened to withstand the extra thrust from the new stone vaults.

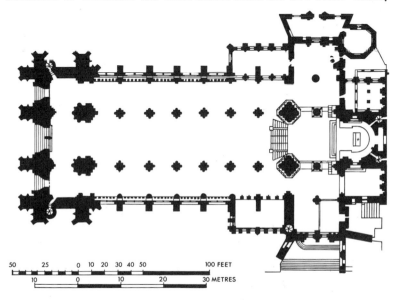

Above, a side view of the cathedral, which displays an overall harmony and balance despite the changeover from Romanesque to Gothic styles: the solid geometry of transepts and dome is echoed in the ample dimensions of the nave windows and balanced by the rectilinear bulk of the west front.

Left, a plan of Strasbourg Cathedral. Note the close juxtaposition of chapels at the east end and the lack of choir. The chapels west of the transepts are late medieval additions.

Far left, an imaginary perspective drawing (c. 1285) of Project B, a design for the façade of the cathedral, executed in the masons' lodge at Strasbourg, later the principal lodge in Central Europe. It demonstrates an understanding of geometry and proportion unparalleled at the time.

179

The next building phase from 1190–1240 included the alteration and enlargement of the crypt and apse, the construction of the north transept, crossing and dome, St Andrew's Chapel to the south of the apse, and the south transept up to half its height—all in a style that was still heavy and Romanesque. The domestic buildings of the monks were then built around a cloister ranged at the east end.

In 1225 a new master-mason of unusual ability took over, perhaps one of two Rudolphs father and son, who introduced the Gothic style. First he erected the Chapel of St John the Baptist to the north of the apse and completed the south transept; then, in 1240, he proceeded on to the nave and the beautiful choir screen (of which only fragments survive). By 1275 the vaults were finished, the nave walled up and Wernher's façade ready to be demolished.

In 1277, the new façade was started. It is traditionally credited to Erwin von Steinbach, though his name is not mentioned until 1284, by when there seem to have already been two unidentified designs. Even the beautiful design known as Project B may not be his, though this was in fact carried out with minor revisions (except for the rose) to the level of the second gallery. There is however a fourth design (known only through a 17th-century copy) bearing Erwin's name; this shows the addition of openwork arcading, openwork gables in the lateral portals and the doubling of tracery in the rose window—which was also lowered—all of which appear in the executed building. Erwin was also probably responsible for introducing the extensive programme of sculpture on the west front. Fire damage must have delayed work on the façade, which was only finally completed by Jean Gerlach (1341–71), who continued the towers up to the platform. The Gallery of the Apostles—which is, unfortunately, extremely close to the top of the rose—was then added. A further regrettable modification was the massive belfry that filled the space above the rose window—the work of Michel de Freibourg. A decade late, in 1399, the services of Ulrich von Ensingen, author of the equally remarkable spire of Ulm, were secured and the north steeple completed in its octagonal stage by 1419. Finally, the spire was added to a new design by Johann Hültz of Cologne and in 1439 the cross was placed at its summit.

Work still continued on the cathedral. In 1485 the pulpit made for the celebrated preacher Geiler de Kayserburg was carved by Hans Hammerer; then between 1495–1521 the area south of the north transept was extended by Jacques de Landshut to form the chapel and remarkable portal of St Laurence, followed by that of St Martin.

Above, the 'jew's harp stringing of Strasbourg' —an independent screen of tracery—enriches and at the same time etherealises the cathedral. A further layer formed by the gable and pinnacles overlaps the tracery of the superlative rose.

Built in the dark pink sandstone of Alsace, Strasbourg Cathedral, opposite, rises above the city—an uncanny and awe-inspiring image. Every element reflects the tension of its striving after height. Yet there is a classical harmony in the basic proportions.

181

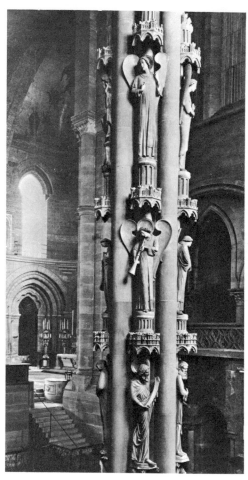

Above, part of the unusual Judgement or Angel Pillar, which stands appropriately in the south transept, where the mystery plays were performed and on whose steps the bishop's tribunals were held.

Above left, the majestic nave of Strasbourg, set against the vast bulwark of the apse and ablaze with prophets, saints and kings as well as the sparkle of storeyed glass.

182

Strasbourg continued to flourish during the Reformation, though unfortunately when the cathedral became Protestant in 1561, large numbers of tombstones and figures of saints and of the Virgin were removed and more than forty altars disappeared. The resulting starkness, even gloom, still persist today. On the annexation of Strasbourg by France in 1681, the cathedral reverted to Catholicism, but further losses took place during the Revolution, when 235 statues on the exterior were destroyed. Even the steeple was threatened by the edict of 1794 ordering the dismantling of all church towers and spires. Indeed, one city councillor declared that it was a contravention of the principle of equality. Luckily a happy compromise was reached: a *bonnet rouge* made of iron was placed on the summit.

Throughout this lengthy building history a wonderful continuity was maintained. This is especially apparent in the interior. The sense of stability in the design of the eastern parts finds a counterpart in the broad dimensions of the nave, which is far less lofty than the French cathedrals of the time. Its elevation is in fact based on that of an equilateral triangle, of which the determining dimension is the width of the nave and aisles, themselves determined by Wernher's foundations. The vertical dimensions of the nave can also be traced back to earlier work. Begun in 1240 the vaults took up the height of those in the south transept, completed shortly after 1230. These in turn were built to match those of the earlier north transept. The nave seems to be about 20 feet higher than that of Wernher's church, whose corbels are probably those seen below the three colonettes supporting the vault of the most eastern bay of the nave.

This increase in height is of course in keeping with the development of the time; indeed the nave of Strasbourg reflects the very latest trends in French design in its lucid and unified combination of clerestory and glazed triforium and its uninterrupted vaulting shafts shooting from floor to vaults. Yet the nave at Strasbourg has a very special majesty of its own, largely created by its breadth; also contributing to this impression are the ranks of patriarchs and prophets that glow from the windows above and of emperors who blaze from the north aisle below.

This majestic impression is enhanced by the choir—a massive apse of masonry rising beyond a vast flight of steps. Built in the pink-grey sandstone of Alsace (grown sombre with time) and ranged with holy figures barely perceptible in the dim light, it evokes the terrifying mystery and drama of Wernher's age. This feeling is particularly noticeable in the two chapels of St Andrew and St John

Above, the Synagogue (c. 1250), a poignant blindfolded figure, with broken staff and dropped tablets.

Far left, the death of the Virgin (c. 1250),whose intense expressions and excited jagged movements anticipate later German art; yet the drapery and its relationship to the body is clearly antique in inspiration.

183

the Baptist. These are almost screened from the transepts, have very low vaulting and their decoration is confined to simple abstract carving on the capitals. Even in the later, south transept, completed in the mid-13th century, the heaviness of the Romanesque still prevails, although a lighter and more animated note has been introduced in the free-standing ensemble of sculpture at the centre known as the Judgement Pillar.

This pier, which supports the eight ribs of the vault, is decorated with three tiers of figures. At the bottom are the four evangelists bearded and robed with expressions of gentle concern. Above them are the four angels of the Last Trump, their heads tilted, their bodies twisting and their wings about to unfold as they prepare to sound their horns, while at the top is Christ as Judge, his face a mirror of compassion, surrounded by three more angels holding the instruments of his Passion. Such a festive spirit—with even a touch of folk art—is unique in the treatment of the Last Judgement; the free-standing form too is without an obvious precedent.

Outside on the steps of the south transept, within view of the Judgement Pillar, the bishops held their tribunals. Here the theme of the sculpture is the Law, old and new. The central figure is King Solomon, dispenser of the old order, and from him rises Christ, the originator of the new. To the right and left are the figures of the Synagogue and the Church, sisters of St Modeste at Chartres. Both have an equal grace and dignity, though the face of the Synagogue is cast down and blindfold while the gaze that the Church directs at her is confident and perhaps a little indulgent. The theme is elaborated in the two rose windows above, in which medallions set in concentric circles tell, on the left, of the superiority of the virtues of the new order over the sacrifices of the old, on the right. The tympana are dedicated to a different theme, that of the Virgin. In the scene of her death the same finely drawn folds and classical inspiration found in the Judgement Pillar betray the presence of a band of craftsmen who arrived at Strasbourg in 1225 after working on the transept porches of Chartres. But infused into this is a pathos scarcely seen before in the middle ages. All the intensity and anxiety of German art from Dürer to Nolde is already evident in the jagged movements and venerable heads of these figures.

The same fervour appears in the figures of the west front. On the north portal the virtues transfix and trample with merciless abandon the vices at their feet. In the centre portal the prophets are expressive

to the point of caricature, some of the figures recalling the nightmare

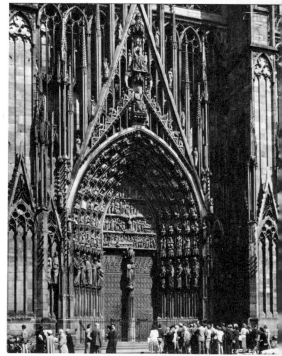

features of the wizard Dr Caligari. And in the right-hand portal the Foolish Virgins smiling vapidly, their lamps cast down, sway at the invitation of their jocular prince, who tempts them with the age-old device of an apple. Opposite them are the Wise Virgins, their lamps help upright, ready to follow the Bridegroom into the sanctuary—the only serene figures of the façade. Such prominence had never been given to this subject before; it was usually treated as a gloss on the great theme of the Last Judgement. Here, represented life-size and in contemporary costume, its message must have been immediately appreciated. Indeed, the general arrangement of the sculpture on the west front is as methodically worked out as that of any of the great cathedrals of the Ile de France.

Later sculpture took the form of decorative embellishments. In 1340 the Chapel of St Catherine was built by Jean Gerlach—a composition at once simple and sophisticated in which piers shoot upwards in a single leap to form an open web of curves and counter-curves on the vaults; the only enrichment is the figures that adorn the piers, headed by canopies even taller and more slender than themselves. These are repeated on a vertiginous scale in the windows behind, executed in silver stain against alternatively red and blue grounds. In the later St Laurence Portal (1495–1505), the many ogee curves are foiled by curious little arcs, which cross each other and terminate abruptly. A similar motif, recalling doodles with a pen and compass, runs below the balustrade; it is also found underneath the canopy combined with foliage as resilient as a spring coil. Certainly there was no decline in decorative resource or design power in the later middle ages.

The medieval glass of Strasbourg, although not quite of the same quality and interest as the sculpture, is equally plentiful. It extends from the second half of the 12th century to the 15th, while there is modern glass in the triforium. Among the earliest (mostly found in the transepts, but considerably rearranged), we should mention the two rose windows of 1230–40 and the window of St Christopher, a giant of 24 feet. The later glass in the five bays of the south aisle depict narrative subjects: the childhood of the Virgin and of Christ next to the crossing followed by the ministry of Christ, an especially beautiful scene representing the miracle of the loaves; next is the Passion of Christ. (All these windows are remarkable for the diamond-patterning of the skies.) The fourth window covers the period from Christ's descent into Hell to the coming of the Holy Spirit, in which the scenes take on a greater breadth. A new expressiveness appears

Top left, the Foolish Virgins (c. 1280) whose unwatchfulness is suggested by their flirtatious attitudes and contemporary costume. Below them are the signs of the Zodiac and occupations of the months (c. 1280).

Bottom left, the centre portal, which between Solomon's throne (on the gable) and Christ's Passion (on the tympanum) unfolds an encyclopedic history of the world.

Below, the portal of St Laurence (1495–1505), typifying the inventiveness of the late middle ages. Note, for instance, the canopy of crossed inverse ogee arches and the motif of compass doodles.

185

in the Hell episodes, where the Devil in chains occupies a whole panel to himself and the backgrounds blaze in a ruby red. The colour is repeated most effectively in the depiction of the Damned in the final window, of which three lancets are devoted to the Last Judgement, a vision of Dantesque power. The theme continues in the narthex, where it forms part of the programme of sculpture belonging to the south portal. Along the opposite aisle is the triumphant procession of the kings and emperors (already mentioned), impressive Byzantine-looking figures outlined in heavy leading and glowing with ruby, ochre and ultramarine and framed in borders like mother-of-pearl. The same kings and emperors appear as equestrian statues along the first gallery encircling the towers.

These towers act as guardians, as it were, to the chief glory of Strasbourg—the steeple—a structure as daring and presumptuous as the original Tower of Babel. Project B provided only for truncated towers according to the latest trend in French design. Less than a century later, Jean Gerlach was planning spires of 380 feet when the Black Death intervened and put an end to his dreams. When initiative was recovered, no attempt was made to build both steeples simultaneously; the aim was to construct a single steeple as tall as possible as quickly as possible. The fact that it was never balanced by a companion (in spite of three attempts to do so at different periods) causes us no disappointment today. We have only to glance at the twin spires of Cologne to realise how more poignant is Strasbourg's single cry to heaven.

The spire soars like a natural growth and every element of the design from the platform to its dizzy summit is calculated to convey this. The lower storey springs upwards in a single bound, one and a half times higher than the windows of the façade below; the more modest upper storey consolidates this leap, while the openwork staircase turrets rise in a single ascent to the base of the spire. Here the feeling of organic growth is even more remarkable. Not only is each little openwork turret taller than that on the tier below but, with their connecting screens, provide the overall motif of the spire, their hexagonal shapes suggesting the cellular formations of nature.

The spire is the supreme example of the harmony of parts described with such enthusiasm by Goethe. Indeed, in his view, however diverse the details of the building may be, they need no system of proportions like that of classical art, for they have been infused by a single creative spirit into a living whole. The same may be said of any great Gothic cathedral.

Further reading list

Aubert, Marcel (ed.), *Petits monographes des Grands Edifices de la France*; Paris
Bowie, T., *The Sketchbook of Villard de Honnecourt*; New York, 1959
Focillon, Henri, *Art of the West in the Middle Ages*, 2 vols; London, 1963
Frankl, Paul, *Gothic Architecture*; London, 1962
Gimpel, Jean, *The Cathedral Builders*; New York, 1961
Harvey, John, *English Cathedrals*; London, 1961
Mâle, Emile, *The Gothic Image*; London, 1961
Panofsky, Erwin, *Gothic Architecture and Scholasticism*; New York, 1962
Pevsner, Nikolaus, *The Buildings of England* series; London

Glossary

abrasion: the grinding away with a wheel of a layer or 'flash' of ruby or other coloured glass.

ballflower: an ornament of the Decorated period consisting of a three-petalled flower enclosing a ball.

bay: the vertical unit between piers or buttresses; also the compartment of a nave or aisle.

Churrigueresque style: a Spanish style of the Baroque period, perhaps partly inspired by the native art of Central and South America and created by José Churriguera and his family.

clerestory: the top storey, pierced by windows, rising above the aisle roofs.

crocket: foliage projections appearing at regular intervals from spires, pinnacles and gables.

cusping: pointed projections formed by the intersection of foils in Gothic tracery.

dog tooth: an Early English ornament consisting of a series of four-pointed stars, pyramidal in section.

fillet: a slim, flat, projecting band running down a shaft or roll moulding.

foil: a lobe formed on the inside of an arch or circle by two arcs of smaller radius. The number of foils is indicated by a prefix, e.g. trefoil.

gallery: an arcaded passage covering the aisle vaults and opening on to the nave.

herm: a three-quarter-length figure on a pedestal used as a decorative motif in Renaissance and later architecture.

jamb: the vertical side of an archway.

lancet: a tall window without tracery.

lierne vault: a vault that includes (as well as structural ribs) decorative or lierne ribs unconnected with the wall supports or central boss.

mullion: a vertical division of a window.

narthex: an antechurch at the main entrance to a church; sometimes called a galilee.

opus alexandrinum: paving of coloured marbles laid in geometrical patterns.

presbytery: the part of a church lying between the choir stalls and the high altar.

putti: representations of infants used as a decorative motif in Renaissance and later architecture.

sedilia: seats for the clergy in the south wall of the chancel.

stiff leaf: an Early English type of foliage resembling the unfurling of bracken.

tabernacle: a free standing canopy supported by columns.

tracery: the intersecting ribwork dividing the lights in the head of a window.

triforium: an arcade wall passage above the nave arcade (and gallery if present) below the clerestory.

trumeau: vertical post supporting the tympanum of a doorway.

tympanum: the area above the lintel enclosed by the arch of a doorway.

voussoirs: the wedge-shaped components of an arch.

187

Index

Acknowledgements

Key to picture positions: (*T*) top, (*B*) bottom, (*L*) left, (*R*) right. Numbers refer to the pages on which the pictures appear.

Aerofilms Ltd. 137, 152; Archives Photographiques 96, 100, 179(*R*), 182(*TL*); Bavaria-Verlag 96, 185; Bildarchiv Foto Marburg 15, 20, 22(*R*), 72(*L*), 127(*L*), 127(*R*), 169(*T*), 182(*B*); Jean Bottin 47; Boudot-Lamotte 39, 61(*T*), 107, 124, 126, 158, 167, 174(*L*); British Museum 10(*T*), 10(*B*), 24(*R*), 25(*L*), 25(*R*), 101(*L*); British Travel Association 135; Bulloz 17(*L*); J. Allan Cash 166; Courtauld Institute of Art 18, 159, 169(*B*), 172; F. H. Crossley 38, 159; Kerry Dundas 129(*L*); French Government Tourist Office 53(*L*), 184(*B*); Giraudon 11, 24(*L*), 27, 67(*R*), 70(*R*), 93, 168(*R*), 171; Peter Goodliffe 153, 175; Paul Hamlyn Library 98(*R*), 112; Michael Holford endpapers, 40, 42(*L*), 43, 44, 45, 46, 48–51, 53(*R*), 54, 55, 56(*T*), 56(*B*), 58–60, 62, 63, 66–67(*B*), 68, 69, 70(*L*), 72(*R*), 73, 74, 76, 77(*T*), 77(*B*), 80(*L*), 80(*R*), 92, 95, 98(*L*), 101(*R*), 102(*L*), 103, 104, 105, 109, 110, 111, 113(*L*), 114–17, 118(*T*), 118(*B*), 119; 120, 138; Italian Cultural Institute 22(*L*); A. F. Kersting 29, 30(*L*), 30(*R*), 31, 33(*T*), 33(*B*), 34, 35(*L*), 35(*R*), 83, 88(*L*), 123, 125, 139, 140, 142–6, 147(*T*), 147(*B*), 148, 149, 155, 156, 157(*L*), 157(*R*), 160(*B*), 161, 163, 165, 174(*R*); Mansell–Alinari 61(*B*); MAS 170; Ministry of Public Building and Works 12(*R*); National Gallery 4; National Monuments Record 160(*T*) (Crown Copyright); Picturepoint 37, 130, 141(*R*); Popperfoto 129(*R*), 184(*T*); H. Roger-Viollet (Hurault-Viollet) 181; Rapho-Doisneau 65; Rapho-Larrier 180; Jean Roubier 14, 84, 106, 173(*L*), 173(*R*), 182 (*TR*), 183; Scala 177; Société des Amis de la Cathédrale de Strasbourg 178; SPADEM photo Chevojon 94; Dr. Franz Stoedtner (Heinz Klemm) 19; Victoria and Albert Museum photo Michael Holford 138; J. D. Webster 18.